GW00673045
PARIS
PARIS
192

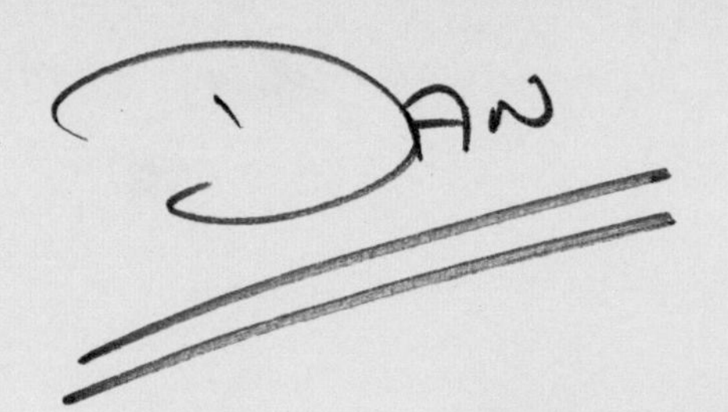

HAPPY TIMES

in the past..

in the present..

in the future..

With all our love
Your friends

Helen and Bryan.

JULY 28 .1974

Other books by Brendan Gill

Death in April

The Trouble of One House

The Day the Money Stopped

Cole

Tallulah

Other books by Jerome Zerbe

People on Parade

El Morocco's Family Album

The Art of Social Climbing

Les Pavillons

Happy

Text by BRENDAN GILL

Photographs by JEROME ZERBE

Harcourt Brace Jovanovich, Inc. NEW YORK

DESIGNED BY PHILIP GRUSHKIN

A portion of the text of this book
appeared in THE NEW YORKER

ISBN 0-15-138480-0

Printed in the United States of America

First edition

BCDE

HAPPY TIMES

The authors acknowledge with gratitude the assistance of Hugh Beeson, Jr., in selecting the photographs for this book. They also thank him for sparing them any work whatever in the compilation of the index.

All of the pictures in this book, with the exception of those in which the photographer himself appears, were taken by Jerome Zerbe.

Everything Happens at Parties

The young and the rich and the beautiful—they have reason, those lucky ones, to wish full records kept of their pleasures and revels, even of their follies. How else are they to outwit the enemy they have in common, implacable time? Documents in the form of words and pictures, but especially pictures, are their means of stating, each in his own way, "Mark me. Envy me. I was this person in this time and place. And I was happy." Memories of good days fail, or are altered by needs unknown in youth, but what the camera registers and preserves unchanged becomes an earnest of immortality. For it is a fact that the camera's eye is able, among many other remarkable things, to stop time; long after the young and the rich and the beautiful are dust, and up to that far-off moment when the last printed image of them is also dust, photographs will bestow on them a posthumous existence, shining with promise. Not the past but the fixed present blazes all round them in its early morning freshness, thanks to the handiwork of someone who, in the course of taking their likenesses, can be said in a sense by no means ironic to have saved their lives.

For forty years, the most industrious lifesaver of this unexpected sort has been an American photographer named Jerome Zerbe. Formidably well-born and well-connected, Zerbe has devoted the greater portion of his career to the depicting of attractive people on delightful occasions—christenings, birthday parties, debuts, weddings, hunt breakfasts, costume balls, cocktail parties, dinner parties, supper parties, yacht races, picnics, clambakes, croquet and tennis matches, theatre openings, and excursions to fashionable resorts and watering places. Christenings and weddings aside, these occasions might strike the historian's eye as trivial; Zerbe would say it was not so, or not necessarily. For the sharers of such occasions are to be seen under their sunniest, most favorable aspect, and this is a fact well worth calling attention to; in practice, we rarely attain the high standard of deportment that we tend to think of as our habitual one. Days of feasting are days of forgiving. Our moments of celebration are almost always kindly as well as courteous. The sorry truth that much of history is an account of mankind at its worst is reason enough to offer as footnotes at the bottom of the page a few glimpses of mankind at its best, or at any rate at its cheeriest. And Zerbe would hold that there are other reasons. It appears, for example, that even this late in the twilight of the twentieth century most of us are brought up with a nineteenth-century puritan distrust of good times, and particularly of other people's good times. Zerbe considers partygiving and partygoing the ideal means of eradicating this sour and miserly emotion. He is a dedicated hedonist, with convictions as strong as any follower of Calvin. To him it is evident that to be joyous, even selfishly joyous, enriches life, while to be despairing, even unselfishly despairing, cheapens it. As Sarah Bernhardt had her gallant "*Quand même*" and Tallulah Bankhead her "Press on!" so Zerbe has his smiling, invariable "Why not?"—a response so characteristic of him that his friend Mrs. William Waldorf Astor recently embroidered it on a pillow, which one catches sight of at once upon entering the drawing room of his apartment on Sutton Place. In Yeats's words, "Hearts are not had as a gift but hearts are earned," and Zerbe holds that a likely place to start earning them is in the merrymaking thick of things, among the dancers and singers and talkers and topers and players of games. It is they, the seemingly profane ones, who turn life into a sacrament by consuming it. They eat, drink, and seize the day, knowing how soon it will end. One could do worse than join them, as Zerbe has always done, out there on the polished ballroom floor, under all those winking crystal prisms and pink balloons. He says with Jane Austen, "Everything happens at parties!" For something *is* always just about to happen on such occasions—an adventure that has the disadvantage for the more cautious among us that we must be willing to assent to it before we have learned its nature. Best to be brave and say "Why not?," then quickly hold out our hands to hands waiting to be taken and drawn close.

Zerbe became this country's first society photographer by chance and it may be that, by the same chance, he will become its last. The reason for his singularity is not that what we think of as "Society" is dying, though its death is announced in newspapers and magazines with tiresome assurance from year to year (in numbers and in amount of wealth, Society is continuously on the increase); the reason is that no other photographer combines, in the Zerbe fashion, exceptional energy with exceptional entrée. Zerbe is no frantic *paparazzo,* hovering outside the gates with strobe light and telephoto lens; his invitation with its gilt coat of arms is tucked in his dinner-jacket pocket, and he makes his way in easy good humor through the gates and up the long drive to the brightly lighted portico in someone's ink-black and almost certainly not rented limousine. His camera is at the ready, but no more significance need be attached to it than to the flower in his buttonhole. Dear Jerry clicking away is first and last dear Jerry. Besides, he has never been known to publish an unfavorable picture; the unlovely negative of a haggard eye, a wrinkled neck, a hand like a claw is at once destroyed. A professional disguised as a gifted, kindly amateur, for decades he has crisscrossed the United States and Europe, moving from great house to great house, from party to party, inexhaustibly. With every evidence of enjoying himself to the fullest, he is forever turning up as a valued guest at Palm Beach, Madrid, Northeast Harbor, Kansas City, Key West, Nassau, New Orleans, Florence, Nantucket, Chicago, Cuernavaca, Gloucester, Deauville, East Hampton, San Francisco, Paris, Oslo, Macon, Akron, London, Versailles, and a hundred towns too small to find their way into atlases but not too small to possess, for Zerbe's pleasure as a connoisseur of architecture, a well-staffed Palladian villa, a honey-colored château, a pillared plantation house behind its stout levee.

Zerbe describes himself as the laziest creature alive, and it is true that one's usual recollection of him is of a big, white-haired, blue-eyed man leaning back on a couch with drink in hand, telling a story, but it is also true that he travels many thousands of miles a year in the course of carrying out his calculatedly unimportant duties as the society editor of *Town & Country,* that he writes and supplies photographs for a column in a magazine called *Palm Beach Illustrated* and that he has recently prepared for publication a sizeable, scholarly work on the pavilions of Europe. He is also engaged in research for a biography of a lifelong favorite, Madame Du Barry. Moreover, his social life is exceptionally strenuous. He lunches and dines out some eight or ten times a week in season, and in Zerbe's set there is always a city or resort somewhere on earth that is just coming into season. He asserts that he has begun to retire as a photographer and that he has already retired as a celebrity. Back in the thirties, he was one of the leading figures in what was then called café society. The local press regularly identified him as the second-handsomest man in New York—one Larry Doyle, a broker and playboy, was reputed to be the handsomest—and a party that Zerbe failed to attend and take pictures of could scarcely claim to have been a party at all; poor devils, without Zerbe the participants were but miserable outsiders, glumly living it up in limbo. Now he affects to believe that he is totally forgotten in New York. The passing of his fame, if it has indeed passed, causes him not the slightest twinge of regret. Looking back, he finds that almost everything that has befallen him has proved fortunate. Perhaps obscurity on his lofty and comfortable level will turn out to have unlooked-for advantages. If it should be so, fine; if not, no matter. Scattered about him in his elegant, dangerously overfurnished apartment ("I have *far* too many things: mind you don't trip") are the fruits of a lifetime of happy work—over a hundred stout scrapbooks containing upwards of fifty thousand photographs. This amounts to an astonishing average of three or four photographs a day every day of every year between 1933 and 1973. As an accumulation of intimate, unpremeditated moments, it becomes a social history unlike any other in the world—a pictorial *roman-fleuve* in which scores of characters are introduced and carried from youth to age, with who they were and what they have become stamped unmistakably upon their faces. Some of the characters are unknown except by their families and close friends; we watch them grow up and grow old in the comparative privacy of houses, country clubs, hotels, and nightclubs. The names of pretty girls change once, then again, and often a third or fourth time. Strangers become friends, become lovers, become husbands, become ex-husbands, become strangers. The men dancing with these elegant women, or lying beside them on the deck of some sloop in the Caribbean—who is to say whether they have been found to be better companions than their predecessors? Practice does not always make perfect, especially in marriage. Others in the large cast of characters in Zerbe's scrapbooks are used to being thought of as members of a cast. They are the innumerable actors and actresses that Zerbe has known and photographed in unrehearsed encounters over the years: the Lunts, Noël Coward, Ina Claire, Gloria Swanson, Tyrone Power, Mary Pickford, Errol Flynn, Ethel Barrymore, Charlie Chaplin, Carole Lombard,

Zerbe with his second camera; the first was a Brownie.

John Garfield, Paulette Goddard, W. C. Fields, Katharine Hepburn, Greta Garbo. We see Shirley Temple grow from a tiny child to a woman in early middle age; Gary Cooper passes from being a fantastically handsome young man at a cocktail party in Hollywood to being a fantastically handsome older man in a sunlit garden in France. The fate we have in common deals with us in different ways; some manage to hold age at bay indefinitely, while others alter so quickly that it is hard to recall what they were like in youth. Cary Grant becomes with every birthday better-looking and more self-confident, while Judy Garland plunges headlong into woeful, puffy-faced decay.

If the scrapbooks are a novel written by a camera, that is because behind the camera has been a man with a novelist's eye and sensibility. It is like Zerbe to be content to leave his enormous work without a formal ending; let it, he says, follow life and peter out untidily whenever and wherever it will. Other matters attract his attention. He is sixty-nine and he has it fixed firmly in mind that he will not live beyond the next year or two. The prospect is by no means distressing; it is simply there for him, as a table or rug is there, and he glances at it from time to time with equanimity. "Mrs. Harvey Cushing said to me once, when she was dying, that dying was a very boring business, and I would hate to be obliged to take a long time over it," Zerbe says. "It's true that I wouldn't have liked being among the first to leave the party, but I'm relieved now not to be among the last. How dreary they are, those greedy hangers-on, squeezing the last moment of pleasure out of things! *Much* nicer to go when one is still capable of saying a proper good-bye." But the metaphor of life as a party irritates him by its expectedness; impatiently, he gestures it aside. "I've drunk a great deal in my life and I've enjoyed it very much, and if drink should kill me, as my doctor keeps telling me it will, I'd consider the bargain a perfectly fair one. But the real reason I talk about dying is to accustom myself to the idea. Most of my old friends—Lucius Beebe, John Perona, Hedda Hopper—are gone. In our youth, we all led lives not calculated to insure extreme longevity. My father survived to almost eighty-nine and my mother to eighty-seven and some of my ancestors hung on into the high nineties, but their habits were, shall we say, different from mine. They thought night was for sleep and day for work, and I suppose they thought play was what was going to happen to them in heaven. *I* think night is for play and day for sleep, and I manage to fit my work into the interstices. I'm certainly not going to live on and on just to please my doctor. Being a cheerful person by nature, I find I am able to think quite cheerful thoughts about my extinction. I read once that the dying brain is calm, and why not? What has it left to get excited over?" He beams and lifts his glass. His blue eyes are merry and his voice is strong. The wind off the East River, freshening, rattles the sashes of the drawing-room windows; the sky is filled with scudding clouds. "To give my doctor *some* satisfaction, I take care to drink as little as possible until dark. One of the nice things about winter in New York is how early it gets dark."

Zerbe was born in a high-gabled wooden country house in Euclid, Ohio, on July 24, 1904. His father, Jerome Brainard Zerbe, for whom he was named, was a prominent citizen and clubman in Cleveland. He was president of the Ohio and Pennsylvania Coal Company, which owned, among other properties, a mine in nearby Cadiz. The most celebrated person ever to be born in Cadiz was the movie star Clark Gable, who in his youth worked in the Zerbe mine. Zerbe and Gable later became friends in Hollywood; one of the bonds between them was a common hatred of mines and mine towns. "They lacked *charm,*" Zerbe says, with a smile that indicates that he and Gable were accustomed to putting the matter more strongly. "The men hated their women. After work, they'd sit around drinking and dreading the time they'd have to go home to their slatternly wives and blackened bungalows. Nobody ever thought to plant a single flower."

The senior Zerbe was fifty-eight at the time of his son's birth, and he celebrated the event as few fathers are able to do, by retiring from business. The Zerbe family is of German origin—the name, pronounced *Zur-bee,* is thought to be a corruption of the place named Zerbst, in Anhalt, East Germany—and settled in this country in the early eighteenth century. Among Zerbe's ancestral connections is a pleasing assortment of Rittenhouses, Rings, Gorgases, Wideners, and the like. Zerbe's mother, twenty-seven years younger than his father, came of a similar background. She had been born Susan Eichelberger, one of several children of a successful railroad lawyer in Urbana, Ohio. Like the Zerbes, the Eichelbergers were of German stock, industrious, ambitious, and notably good-looking. One of Susan's brothers became a lieutenant general in the Second World War and served as Superintendent at West Point; two others were prominent lawyers. Susan Eichelberger's beauty of person and voice was such that when, on a visit to New York at the age of twenty-one, she happened to meet Charles Frohman, he offered to provide her with training and star her in a play.

Zerbe's birthplace in Euclid.

Zerbe's father at eighty-eight.

His offer proved to be a serious one and she accepted it, but made the mistake of telling her family the good news; an uncle was dispatched immediately to bring her back to the trans-Appalachian safety of Urbana. The senior Zerbe, then a widower with a grown daughter, caught sight of Susan Eichelberger at a party in Cleveland and said to a companion, "If that young lady is not married, I'm going to make her my wife." She wasn't and he did. Their first child was a daughter, whom they named Margaret; Jerome, Jr., was born a year later. Margaret's name was early reduced to Maggie and then elevated, by her young brother, into Margot. (Long before he reached his teens, Zerbe liked things to sound stylish and, if possible, French; he was a Francophile from the cradle.) Margot grew up to marry Roy Larsen, Henry Luce's right-hand man in the building of *Time*. "I admire Roy immensely," Zerbe says. "He and Margot and their family—first the children and now the grandchildren as well—have always been *my* family. I don't regret having remained a bachelor. Some of my friends have married as they grew older, for reasons of money or social position or fear of loneliness, but none of these reasons has borne much weight with me. Oh, I've had two or three close calls with marriage, but I've always said, 'Why isn't everything fine the way it is?' There's never any answer to that."

After a brief period in Euclid, the Zerbes moved into a big red-brick mansion in Cleveland, designed for them by the fashionable architect Abram Garfield. Little Jerome attended public school, to which he was driven by the family chauffeur. Every morning as soon as he stepped out of the car, the school bully would dash up and give him a thorough beating. Jerome assumed that this was the nature of the human condition and took his daily beating as bravely as possible, but the chauffeur was upset. He attempted to outwit the bully by dropping Jerome a block or so away from the school and letting him approach it humbly on foot, like most of the other students. This was not as good an idea as it seemed; the bully discovered the ruse and took to waylaying the car and beating up the chauffeur as well as his little master.

Having survived the rigors of his early education in Cleveland, Jerome came east to attend the Salisbury School, in Salisbury, Connecticut. There he began to cultivate a talent for drawing and for writing verse. He was clever at getting a likeness, and his charcoal and pencil sketches of football captains and other prep-school luminaries appeared in the school literary magazine, *Ye Sarum Booke*. So did a number of his poems, which, like the works of most adolescent poets, dwelt with relish on the transient beauties of this world and the welcome prospect of death. As things turned out, death was closer than the young poetaster had supposed; he fell mysteriously ill and was rushed home to Cleveland, where a family friend, the eminent surgeon George Washington Crile, discovered a tuberculous gland in Jerome's neck. The gland was successfully operated on by Dr. Crile, who then recommended that Jerome take a year or so off from his studies to recuperate.

Zerbe's boyhood home in Cleveland.

Where Zerbe held court at Yale.

Jerome, who detested school, considered this an excellent idea. His parents were persuaded to take his sister and him on a leisurely trip abroad; they spent fourteen months touring Italy, the Rhineland, and France, where Jerome was confirmed in his passion for things French. While the Zerbe family was staying on the Riviera, Jerome was invited to spend a weekend with W. Somerset Maugham, at the Villa Mauresque, in Cap Ferrat. "I left sooner than I was expected to," he recollects now. "There was more Byzantine intrigue in the air than I was prepared to cope with at the time. Nothing in Cleveland had prepared me for Willie Maugham. He later became a friend of mine and was amused to learn how uneasy his peculiar household had made me. I took a picture of him in his extreme old age and though I made it as flattering as possible, there was no way to keep him from looking like a diseased thousand-year-old bird of prey."

In 1924, being by then a couple of years older than the average college freshman, Zerbe entered Yale in the class of '28. He took the well-known courses in English literature taught by William Lyon Phelps, John Berdan, and Chauncey Brewster Tinker, joined the Dramat and the *Record,* and drew pictures of his friends. Tinker was an exceptionally ugly man, with a splayed, bulbous nose, a scraggly crew cut worn *en brosse,* and a glass eye that could fix a student more fiercely than any real one. With characteristic softness of heart, Zerbe sketched a likeness of him that Berdan said was how "Tink" was going to be allowed to look in heaven. By senior year, Zerbe was maintaining a distinguished salon in his luxurious quarters on the so-called Gold Coast in Harkness Quadrangle. He had a living room with a wood-burning fireplace, two bedrooms, and a bath, and his furniture, books, linen, and silver were much admired. On his walls hung drawings by Van Dyck, Kneller, and other artists of consequence. (Professor Berdan having told him that the Kneller was far too valuable a work of art for any mere undergraduate to possess, Zerbe obediently presented it to the Elizabethan Club, of which he was not a member.) Football players were prominent frequenters of his salon, in part because they liked him and in part because, themselves hard-driving puritans headed for Wall Street, marriage, and all its attendant responsibilities, they were puzzled by his carefree pagan attitude toward life. They also enjoyed the liquor that, despite Prohibition, Zerbe was able to keep flowing in abundance. "New Haven was a very active port in those days," Zerbe has said. "I had a friend who was a sailor and whenever his ship docked in New Haven he would turn up at Harkness with a case of gin on his shoulder. My friends and I were always very grateful."

"The second most socially prominent member of the class of '28."

The board of The Yale Record, *a humorous publication.*

Having been voted the second-greatest social celebrity in the class of '28 (in first place was Charles Tiffany Bingham, son of the then Governor of Connecticut), as well as the fifth most gentlemanly member of the class, to say nothing of sixth most original and eighth most entertaining, Zerbe graduated and took off with a titled relative—Princess Irma Odescalchi, a niece of his half sister—for his first visit to Hollywood. His intention was to earn a little money drawing portraits of society figures there. Such figures proved in short supply; nevertheless, he succeeded in drawing, at seventy-five dollars a head, likenesses of Cecil B. De Mille, Norma Shearer, and Basil Rathbone, among others in Hollywood's top drawer, and he was lucky enough to meet a couple of promising movie beginners, Lupé Velez and Gary Cooper, who introduced him to the younger and more dashing movie crowd. From then on, for over thirty years, Zerbe was to be a frequent visitor to Hollywood; Cooper aside, among his closest friends in the colony were Hedda Hopper, Cary Grant, Errol Flynn, Randolph Scott, Marion Davies, and Paulette Goddard.

In 1929, at the height of the boom, Zerbe went off to Paris, on an allowance from his father of three hundred dollars a month—a sum sufficient in the Paris of those days to permit the renting of a pleasant flat in the Rue du Bac and the occasional purchase of a fine old drawing or piece of furniture. He enrolled in the Académie Julian, founded by M. Julian, a strict upholder of traditional methods. Zerbe's intention was to become a portrait painter on the order of Sargent; certainly among his friends there were plenty of subjects rich enough and important enough to bestow commissions on a grand scale. Zerbe soon made the acquaintance of Man Ray, Janet Flanner, and other notable American expatriates. ("Jerry did a drawing of me that made me look like a Jewish Lafayette," Miss Flanner has since said. "I was astonished to learn that many people considered it an excellent likeness.") Zerbe also met and consorted with such international society figures as Princess Helena Murat, Count Guido Sommi-Peccenardi, and Baron George Hoynigen-Huene. A gifted and

From the balcony of Zerbe's apartment in Paris.

fashionable photographer of the day, whose work often appeared in *Vanity Fair* and *Vogue,* Hoynigen-Huene encouraged Zerbe's interest in taking pictures instead of drawing them. For it was the case that the longer Zerbe frequented Julian's atelier, the less confident he was of becoming a second Sargent. Moreover, it appeared that he would rather play than work—if his talent was considerable, it was not in the least overbearing and so made the smallest possible demands upon his discipline. He was plainly not going to give all to art; faced with a choice between it and good times, he would quickly choose good times. Zerbe began to perceive that for him the great advantage of photography was that by means of it he could hope to marry his vocation to his avocation. His vocation was partygiving and partygoing and his avocation was making a record of these parties in his diaries and neatly captioned black imitation-leather scrapbooks. He was like Proust in having the air of a social butterfly and the instincts of a historian; he might stay up all night dancing and drinking, but he never went to bed without scrupulously jotting down a few salient notes on where he had been and whom he had seen. It is a habit he continues to this day. After a couple of years of contented sketching and idling in Paris, Zerbe was summoned home to Cleveland. Thanks to the Depression, his father's coal mines were no longer profitable, and it was thought that the time had come for the young heir to put his shoulder to the wheel. The wheel would certainly not consist of digging coal, but everyone in the family agreed that it would be helpful at this moment of moderate impoverishment (even the family cook and chauffeur were feeling moderately impoverished) if Jerry could think of *some*thing constructive to do. His brother-in-law, Roy Larsen, was rising in the world in pleasing exact concordance with the meteoric rise of *Time,* while Jerry was, it appeared, simply bobbing. By good luck, a boyhood companion of his, Winsor French, had been planning for some time to start a weekly magazine in Cleveland that would bring to that rather grim industrial city some of the sunny cultural attributes of *Vanity Fair* and *The New Yorker.* Having acquired a backer, W. Walter White, who played polo and whose only stipulation was that he be allowed to write the polo news, French asked Zerbe to help launch the magazine. It was called *Parade,* and Zerbe was given the title of art director. In practice, this meant that he drew pictures for the magazine, wrote for it, and took photographs for it of various social events in Cleveland. In those days, private parties were truly private; reporters and photographers were not expected to mingle with guests. Nor did society matrons allow their pictures to appear in newspapers and magazines, for the rule was still roughly that of the Victorian period: a woman's name was expected to appear in print only three times—at her birth, at her wedding, and at her death. Zerbe soon changed the rules for Cleveland, as he was later to do for New York and the country at large. He persuaded some of the leading society matrons to pose for *Parade,* usually on the pretext that the publication of their photographs would help bring attention to some favored philanthropy of theirs; once the leaders had established a precedent, Zerbe's makeshift studio was besieged by lesser matrons, all of them eager to see their faces in *Parade.* As for his snapping pictures at parties—not an inconspicuous thing to do with the heavy cameras and enormous, unreliable flashbulbs then in use—the fact was that he would have been invited to attend the party as a Zerbe and not as a member of the press, and he was, besides, always agreeably bent upon giving other people pleasure. Indeed, he was so often the life of the party that no hostess could afford to send him and his camera away.

Despite the Depression and the many thousands of people out of work in Cleveland in the early thirties, Society went on giving substantial parties.

Baron George Hoyningen-Huene.

Zerbe remembers that a friend of his said of her daughter's forthcoming debut, "I want to keep it simple, even if it costs me a million," and to him this remark epitomizes the spirit of the Clevelanders among whom he grew up and from whom he took his earliest social attitudes. Great fortunes had begun to be accumulated in Cleveland in the nineteenth century. Some of the new rich—the Rockefellers, the Whitneys, the Harknesses—came east to New York, but many other new-rich families—the Hannas, the Severances, the McKinneys—were content to remain in Cleveland and become, with customary Middle Western celerity, old rich. Zerbe's father had been able but unambitious in business (he spent the last thirty years of his life playing bridge with cronies at the Union Club in Cleveland), and the result was that the Zerbes never got beyond being what used to be known as "well-fixed." Long before the Depression, they had sold their big Georgian house to members of the Halle family. In seeking smaller and more manageable quarters, Mrs. Zerbe had announced, to her son's alarm, that she intended to purchase "the ugliest house in Cleveland." In fact, it proved to be a charming turn-of-the-century Queen Anne house with ample rooms and an immense porch that, in summer, would be transformed into an airy outdoor drawing room of unexpected elegance, furnished with fine French pieces and having at one end, to shield it from the street and from inclement weather, a very large four-paneled screen that Zerbe painted to resemble an aquarium, filled with unlikely fishes.

He had more and more time to paint and draw, because *Parade,* for lack of sufficient advertising revenue, was racing to an end. Zerbe's father died in 1933, and for a while Zerbe considered taking personal charge of the family company. A visit to the mine at Cadiz, which led to his observing at firsthand the conditions under which the miners worked, at a depth of almost nine hundred feet and with the mine face almost three miles from the entrance shaft, renewed his conviction that business, and especially the coal business, was not for him. By then, his informal society pictures in *Parade* had caught the attention of Harry Bull, editor of *Town & Country,* in New York. Bull perceived that Zerbe's camaraderie with his subjects and his novelist's eye for the telling background detail had introduced something new into society reporting. Bull published some of the Cleveland pictures and commissioned Zerbe to cover for *Town & Country* notable social events in Detroit, Chicago, and elsewhere in the Middle West.

Once *Parade* was defunct, there was only family to bind Zerbe to Cleveland. He began to wonder whether his destiny might not lie in the far bigger and more amusing playground of Manhattan, and it was a classic minor family skirmish that prompted him to risk taking the bold step eastward. He had made the acquaintance of Max Schmeling, the former heavyweight boxing champion of the world. Schmeling was visiting friends in Cleveland, and one day Zerbe invited

Dummies at the Académie Julian.

him to the house for cocktails. Later that evening, Mrs. Zerbe informed her son, "I don't wish to entertain prize fighters in my home." Zerbe said, " 'In *my* home'? I thought it was *our* home." Shortly thereafter, having supplied himself with a nest egg of a few hundred dollars by the sale of his collection of art books to the Cleveland Museum of Art and having secured from Bull the promise of a salary of a hundred and fifty dollars a month for his photographic services to *Town & Country,* Zerbe packed his paints and cameras into his old Buick and took off for New York. Though his parting with his mother was amicable—she arranged for him to be given a small allowance from his father's estate—her friends were quick to assure Zerbe that his leaving Cleveland would be the death of her. On the contrary, within a year Zerbe had persuaded her to come to New York for a long visit, which she was to repeat regularly for the rest of her life; and she often said that her son's moving to New York was one of the most fortunate turning points in her life—hadn't she, after all, as a girl of twenty-one, intended to take the city by storm?

Zerbe rented a small apartment in a brownstone at 62 East Fifty-sixth Street, at a rental of sixty dollars a month. (Curiously, he has spent his life in New York entirely on East Fifty-sixth Street. Following a couple of years in Number 62, he moved across the street to Number 59, and when, after twenty-four years, the building was thrown down to make way for an addition to the Drake Hotel, he moved into his present apartment in the building on the northwest corner of Fifty-sixth Street and Sutton Place.) Within a few weeks of his arrival in New York, Zerbe was offered a job at the Rainbow Room, at the top of the RCA Building in Rockefeller Center; suavely designed and with a spectacular view out over the city and its labyrinth of rivers and bays, the restaurant-nightclub was then but a year or so old and much in need of publicity. The management counted on Zerbe's knack for "dressing" a room with people of the right sort; he would be paid seventy-five dollars a week for three evenings a week, in the course of which, at no expense to him, he was to give agreeable dinner parties for fashionable friends, take their pictures, and then see to it that the pictures got to the newspapers and press associations. At the time, there were seven newspapers and three press associations in New York and they had plenty of space for pictures of society folk at play. Zerbe has always been puzzled by the fact that throughout the grim period of the Depression the sorely beset poor and even the unemployed seemed to take pleasure in pictures of the rich squandering their unearned incomes upon frivolity. "I'd have expected my pictures to make people furious," he has said. "They had just the opposite effect. My friends and I were all more or less Marie Antoinettes in our attitudes, but instead of having our heads chopped off, we were applauded. Very strange. As for myself, if there *had* been a revolution, I'd have acted like my favored heroine in history, Madame Du Barry—I'd have screamed, howled, and wept every inch of the way to the guillotine."

By way of celebrating his pleasant deal with the Rainbow Room, Zerbe stopped off at the nightclub El Morocco to have a drink with his friend John Perona, who owned it. Perona was indignant with himself for having failed to think of employing Zerbe's talents in such a straightforwardly devious way and at once offered him a job on the same terms—seventy-five dollars a week for three of the four remaining evenings in Zerbe's week, along with unlimited food and drink for him and his friends. Soon Zerbe's pictures of socialites and celebrities were turning up in newspapers and magazines from coast to coast, and Perona decided to secure his services on an exclusive basis (*Town & Country* aside), paying him a hundred and fifty dollars a week, plus expenses, for a full seven-day week. The new

Max Schmeling on the Zerbes' porch in Cleveland.

arrangement was less arduous and more amusing than the old, for somehow the Rainbow Room could not readily free itself of the Baptist taint of its owners, the Rockefellers. Thus it befell that from 1933 to 1938, nearly every night of Zerbe's life between nine and four in the morning was spent at El Morocco, eating, drinking, dancing, gossiping, and, with a never-diminished zest, incessantly taking pictures.

In the thirties, El Morocco was considered the most exclusive nightclub in the city. Its rival, the Stork Club, was presided over by a former Oklahoma farm boy and bootlegger named Sherman Billingsley, who, unlike Perona, tended to show a proud disdain for fiscal prudence. He cultivated the rich in the way that they have always secretly liked best, by seeming to save them money. No debutante or personable young couple ever had to pick up a tab at the Stork, and it was literally the case that gifts of perfume, cigarettes, stockings, scarves, and even hundred-dollar bills would come floating through the air and stream down upon the tables. Zerbe makes a simple distinction between El Morocco and the Stork—"one had class and the other didn't." El Morocco was *the* place to be seen, especially after the theatre. A queue of well-born, well-heeled people, all armed with reservations, would be willing to stand for long periods in the street until they could gain admission to the sacred place; a visitor to the city in those dark thirties days might easily have assumed that they were among our masses of patiently waiting unemployed. "Not to be able to get a table at El Morocco was a terrible blow to people's egos," Zerbe says. "Grown men would break down with frustration at failing to catch the eye of Carino, the maître d'. I don't know how many thousands of pictures I took at El Morocco. Except in the case of a person committing some marital or other indiscretion, nobody ever asked me *not* to take a picture. They were there to show off in front of each other and they didn't mind showing off before the whole world as well. Mind? They wore the small fame I gave them as if it were a badge."

When El Morocco was built, in 1932, the decorator Vernon McFarlane chose an extraordinary imitation zebraskin covering for the banquettes, and many people afterward supposed that the choice had been made in order to assure an immediate identification of the club in photographs. Not at all, for when the stripes went on, nobody was taking pictures in nightclubs for distribution to the press. Zerbe was a year away from

Zerbe's mother served coffee every afternoon at three-thirty.

inventing this singular and highly successful form of public relations, and it was only by chance that McFarlane provided a background for Zerbe's handiwork so vivid and unmistakable that it was soon to be recognized all over the world and to provide, for strangers who were perhaps never to visit this country, a quintessential glimpse of chic Manhattan night life. (Lacking such ready means of identification, the Stork fell back upon the large black ceramic ashtrays with the words "The Stork Club" boldly inscribed on them in white. Nearly every picture taken at the Stork over the years had an ashtray prominently displayed in the foreground, with the presumed subjects of the picture smiling away rather dimly in the background.)

Thanks to Zerbe's many friendships with people in high places, a number of aristocrats appeared at El Morocco who had never before visited a nightclub. The undisputed *grande dame* of New York Society at the time, Mrs. Cornelius Vanderbilt, turned up on several occasions and was not unamused. Zerbe liked to keep a shrewd mixture of socialites, actors, athletes, and well-known figures in the arts flowing in an unbroken profusion of candid snapshots to the press. To help preserve this continuity, one very important lady, Mrs. William K. Vanderbilt, would come to the club carrying a half-dozen hats; Zerbe would photograph her in one hat after another and would then release the pictures over a period of weeks, giving the impression that Mrs. Vanderbilt was regularly dropping in at El Morocco, when in fact she would long since have departed for Deauville, Palm Beach, or some other agreeable outpost of civilization. "The thing to be remembered about El Morocco is that we all had so much genuine fun there," Zerbe says. "Not just café society, but people of some importance in the world, who, it strikes me now, were more given to playfulness after hours than people today. Men like Benchley, Harold Ross, Jock Whitney—why, even Henry Luce, egged on by Clare, managed to have good times at the club. John Perona was one of the best hosts in the world, as well as one of my closest friends. An extraordinary man! He was born of peasant stock in northern Italy and set out at sixteen to make his way in the world. Reaching England, he signed on as a deck hand on an ocean liner. He spent his last night ashore with a girl, lost track of time, and failed to catch the boat train to Southampton. The ship he missed was the *Titanic*. He later sailed on the old *Homeric* for South America. He was bullied by the crew and, hating it, jumped ship in Buenos Aires. There he became a boxer, built up his body, and earned a living as a sparring partner. He worked his way to New York and got a job as a busboy in the old Knickerbocker Grill. His good looks appealed to everyone and he soon saved enough from his salary to open a small restaurant on Broadway. One day in the street he ran into a man he had sparred with in South America and invited him to have all his meals at Perona's. His name was Luis Angel Firpo. So when the press asked Firpo where he was going to celebrate on the historic night that he knocked Jack Dempsey out of the ring, Firpo said, 'At Perona's! The best food in town!' John's career was made. All the sports people flocked to his place. During Prohibition, he ran a couple of speakeasies, including the Bath Club, and he had El Morocco ready to open the moment repeal came. What energy he had, and what a lot of pleasure he got out of life! At four in the morning, we'd leave the club—it was at 154 East Fifty-fourth Street in those days—and John would have arranged to have as many as four cabs lined up at the curb, their motors running, and in every cab there'd be a pretty girl. John would look them over and then choose one to take home with him, or more often two. He and Errol Flynn and Aly Khan and Rubirosa—I knew them all well, and of their kind I would have to call them heroic."

Zerbe not only photographed celebrities but in the course of doing so became a celebrity himself. He was constantly written about in the press, especially by Cholly Knickerbocker, whose assorted society columns for the Hearst syndicate appeared locally in the *Journal* (later the *Journal-American*), and by Lucius Beebe, whose syndicated column, "This New York," appeared locally in the *Herald Tribune*. Cholly Knickerbocker was the pseudonym of a short, fat, heavily perfumed, squeaky-voiced, and irascible arbiter of both café society (a term he claimed to have invented and always wrote of in upper case) and of Society at large, whose real name was Maury H. B. Paul. In his day, his often savagely worded decisions as to who constituted Society were much feared, and he took an outsider's relish in prompting fears. He was of obscure origin, perhaps a generation away from some miserable European ghetto, and in saying that his real name was Maury H. B. Paul one risks repeating a fiction of his own devising. The name Paul happens to have pleasing social resonances in Philadelphia, but Maury Paul's Pauls were unknown; he pretended otherwise and to clinch the case for his aristocratic background he asserted that his middle initials stood for Henry Biddle, though no proper Biddle would ever acknowledge the relationship. Boldness is all, especially when it comes to forging genealogies; Paul's fabrications prospered and his power as Cholly Knickerbocker remained unchallenged. In café society, to be praised by him was the highest boon and to be damned by him was like death. Zerbe was among those who were always praised. As for Beebe, who became an intimate friend, he wrote about Zerbe at such length that Walter Winchell, the leading gossip columnist of the period and a man—illiterate, vituperative, hard-driving—as unlike Beebe as it was possible to be, used to complain publicly in the *Mirror* that Beebe should call his column not "This New York" but "Jerome Never Looked Lovelier."

Beebe was of a type that has almost vanished from the earth. For arbitrariness of opinion and refinement of dress and manners, perhaps only Joseph Alsop, who was a beginning reporter on the *Tribune* in Beebe's glory days, could be said to embody in the present era certain echoes of Beebe's supremely self-confident eccentricity. A Boston brahmin who even in the depths of the Depression granted himself an allowance of a hundred dollars a day for food and drink, Beebe, known to Zerbe in affectionate raillery as "Uncle Horrible," maintained a private railroad car and once covered a fire in a morning coat. In the eyes of his colleagues on the *Tribune*, he was the most unreliable reporter on earth; in a profile of Beebe published in *The New Yorker* in the late thirties, Wolcott Gibbs gave an example of Beebe's casual practice of journalism:

Told to cover a banquet of the New York Central Railroad Engineers, he appeared somehow at one sponsored by the Caledonian Club, and after lingering only long enough to get a prepared copy of the principal speech, went back to his office to report that the President of the Central had incomprehensibly chosen to talk to his men about Scotland. He was astonished by the clamor which the publication of this item aroused, being clearly of the opinion that one damn dull dinner was very much like another.

Unreliability made little difference to his column—it was a hastily hurled-together gallimaufry of trivial items about the rich and wellborn, and the last thing that any devoted Beebe reader required of them was that they be true. Sample items, as cited by Gibbs:

Stanley Sackett pays $7.50 a pair for his French lisle socks. . . . Doris Duke has nine Rolls Royces. . . . Ona Munson's drawing-room is quite littered with pianos. . . . M. André Simon of the Wine and Food Society ordered a a bowl of spring flowers removed because it infringed on the bouquet of the Château Latour '20. . . . Margaret Valdi Curtis, a relative of Lord Asquith, is around town singing Tahitian songs in a straw skirt. . . . Mrs. Graham Fair Vanderbilt's butler is reported to have been dismissed for saying "O.K., Madam." . . . Prince Kyril Scherbatow, A. K. Mills, and this department discovered the other day they were wearing identical suits. Tony Williams is a wretch to have duplicated them on us.

Beebe often stretched English to the breaking point and then grandly broke it. "Ingrained in his character," Gibbs wrote, "there is a profound nostalgia for dead elegance, and his prose is consequently heavy with Gothic ornament. Almost anything on wheels becomes a 'herdic;' a serving dish is a 'firkin;' 'zounds' and 'egad' break up the rolling periods. It is impossible for him to write 'hat' or 'street' or 'policeman.' They are transmuted into '*chapeau*,' '*faubourg*,' and '*gendarme*,' and at one time the Gallic inspiration was so strong upon him that 'success foolish' and 'but incredible' threatened to unseat whatever was left of his readers' minds."

Thanks to the frequent mention of his name in columns, Zerbe was soon invited to bring out a book of his pictures, which he called *People on Parade*. Beebe provided a characteristic introduction, which ran in part:

Jerome Zerbe's photographs are news photographs and why this book has every right to be called a document. Usually "documents," profound, vital "documents," are as dull as a bottle of corked Vouvray, but *People on Parade* is a notable and happy exception.

The customary conception of a news photographer is of a fellow who has to fight like bejezzus [sic] for his living and who wears extra heavy shoes to jam into closing doors. To this, too, Mr. Zerbe is an exception. In an atmosphere of seagoing dowagers and hot and cold running footmen where elegance and potted rubber plants are the watchword he lolls, metaphorically, in Babylonish ease while flunkies flood him with Châteauneuf-du-Pape and firkins of fish eggs are wheeled by at frequent intervals.

The very nature of Mr. Zerbe's photographs makes calculated photographic effects at once superfluous and impossible. They are news pictures of a highly specialized sort, showing elegant or famous or witty people in brief instants of parade or pleasure, sometimes in juxtapositions which, to the sapient, are hilarious. . . . Mostly, like Mr. Robinson's Richard Corey, people glitter as they walk through the pages of this album and you will probably find yourself among them. If you don't the chances are Mr. Zerbe has heard that you once chilled your claret or saw a play the second night. His code is a rigid one.

Slight as the book was, it earned Zerbe recognition from *Time:* "Always immaculately groomed, with an impressive acquaintance among New York's bright young people, he flashlights all the swankier bars, nightclubs, balls, routs, and receptions. With determination and no little skill Photographer Zerbe has dedicated his life to recording the lives of the champagne set in its moment of abandon."

In 1939, Zerbe accepted the offer of a job as host at the Brazilian Pavilion at the New York World's Fair. In 1940 he moved to a similar position at the Italian Pavilion. Though the grim steps that would lead to the outbreak of the Second World War were already being taken in Europe and Asia, the Fair purported to reveal the peaceful future that mankind by its technological prowess had learned at last how to bring into being. If this was nonsense, and known to be nonsense, the Fair was nevertheless an exceptionally brilliant event of its kind and an exceptionally happy one for the tens of millions of people who passed through its gates. Zerbe entertained at the Fair as if the grounds were his drawing room. Not merely hundreds but thousands of his friends and acquaintances had merry times with him there. One of the most remarkable misadventures to take place during the Fair involved a couple of Jerry's friends and, in a minor role, Jerry himself. It was described in part in a front-page story in the New York *Times*, which unfortunately had to go to press before the misadventure ended. From the *Times* of July 13, 1939:

> An unscheduled thrill drew thousands of persons to the Parachute Jump in the Amusement Zone of the New York World's Fair last night when one of the 'chutes became jammed in mid-air after hauling a man and a woman more than 100 feet towards the top of the 250 ft. tower.
>
> Seated beneath the billowing folds of a huge orange 'chute, which was tipped at a steep slant when one of the pulleys jammed against a supporting wire, the two were visible throughout virtually the entire Fair area. Their only support was the small, swing-like double seat on which they sat side by side, clinging to each other, and held from falling by their safety belts.
>
> The accident that trapped them aloft occurred at 11:25 o'clock.

Among the ten thousand people who were estimated to have gathered at the foot of the jump was the ubiquitous Zerbe. The couple trapped in the parachute had not been identified; Zerbe heard somebody say that the man was thought to be Harold Talbott, a friend of his. He shouted up in the dark, "Are you Harold Talbott?" and the man shouted back, "None of your business!"

Somewhat taken aback, Zerbe said, "But I'm Jerry Zerbe!"

His assumption that everybody in the world either knew him or knew his name and would be glad to speak to him was well founded. Out of the dark came the voice, "Jerry! My God! I'm Cocie Rathborne!"

Another friend, of course: J. Cornelius Rathborne, Yale '31, and a well-known polo player on Long Island. He and his wife—the woman beside him in mid-air—were often to be seen at El Morocco. Mrs. Rathborne, though admirably calm in her dangerous plight, was under the impression that she and her husband might fall and be killed before being rescued. She called down to Zerbe, "This is one time I wish you had your camera. Our picture would be something for the children to have." Zerbe assured them that they would soon be safely on the ground. A free-lance newspaper photographer near Zerbe was eager to get a picture of the trapped couple at close range but was afraid to risk going up in an adjacent parachute for fear that it, too, might jam. Moreover, since he had but a single flashbulb left, the odds were against his getting a saleable picture even if he *did* go up. Mostly for Mrs. Rathborne's sake, Zerbe volunteered to take the picture for him. A two-hundred-and-thirty-pound policeman was induced to accompany Zerbe for ballast, and up they went, stopping at the same height as the broken parachute. A hundred and ten feet above the ground, Zerbe leaned far out into space and was just aiming the camera at his friends when the fat policeman fainted and slumped against him; Zerbe snapped the picture, the flashbulb fortunately went off, and the parachute descended. The poor Rathbornes remained trapped in the air for five hours. The next morning, after a couple of hours' sleep at their home in Old Westbury, they returned and gallantly went up for another ride, in order that the Fair should receive as little unfavorable publicity from the accident as possible. Zerbe's picture turned out to be an excellent one and the photographer sold it to the *Journal-American* for five hundred dollars.

When, in the second year of the Fair, the Italian government declared war on England and France, Zerbe resigned his post at the Italian Pavilion. To show that he felt no personal ill will, he invited all of the pavilion waiters he knew to bring their wives to a party in his apartment on East Fifty-sixth Street. "I was expecting it to be a sad farewell occasion, but not at all," he says. "Most of the men managed to stay on here and wound up as headwaiters in our best restaurants and nightclubs. Some have been friends of mine ever since."

Zerbe devoted the next couple of years to his usual assignments for *Town & Country*. He also made a good deal of money taking advertising photographs; he would drape a couple of well-dressed, good-looking young friends of his along a banister at the St. Regis, or seat them in a country garden beside some babbling fountain, and the text accompanying the photograph would hint that youth, beauty, riches, and a velvety skin were all one and would be found together inside a bottle of Jergens Lotion. In 1942, Zerbe enlisted in the Navy. He could have applied for a commission and, given his connections, he would certainly have received one, but his intention was to be useful as well as decorative, and he had discovered that the Navy had a tradition that no officer ever sank so low as to snap a shutter with his own hands. (Captain Steichen's Navy unit was to be the one exception to this rule.) Since what Zerbe knew best was taking pictures, he willingly signed himself on as a chief photographer's mate. Being an invincible social butterfly—or lion—he soon found himself living the life of an officer. Despite his lowly rank, he was on an equal footing with admirals in the great houses of San Francisco, Burlingame, and Pebble Beach, and with his usual courtesy he looked down as inconspicuously as possible on social-climbing vice admirals and commanders. Eventually, he was assigned to a photographic unit at the headquarters, on the island of Guam, of Admiral Nimitz, the grand panjandrum of the Pacific command. One day Robert E. Sherwood, the distinguished playwright and speech-writer for President Roosevelt, arrived for consultation at Nimitz's quarters. Zerbe was waiting outside in his jeep, ready according to custom to squeeze off a few shots of the latest visiting V.I.P., whoever he might be. Sherwood came out, spotted his old friend Zerbe, and embraced him heartily. As the group prepared to set out on a tour of the island, Sherwood said to Nimitz, "Admiral, if you don't mind, I'd like to ride with my friend Jerry here." The Admiral looked baffled as he gave his consent; how was he—CINCPAC—to consult with Sherwood if Sherwood was bouncing along in a jeep with a chief photographer's mate?

Portraits by Zerbe.

RIGHT, *Regan McKinney.*

BELOW, LEFT, *Winsor French.*

BELOW, RIGHT, *Count Guido Sommi-Peccenardi*

ABOVE, LEFT, *Mrs. Joseph Bryan III.*

ABOVE, RIGHT, *Kay Halle.*

LEFT, *Mrs. Michael Arlen*

Subsequently, and no doubt consequently, Zerbe became Nimitz's personal photographer, and toward the end of the war CINCPAC often tried to bypass naval regulations and have Zerbe made a lieutenant commander by presidential fiat. He sent three messages to the White House to this effect. By what ought to have been good luck but proved to be very bad luck, Franklin D. Roosevelt, Jr., a close friend of Zerbe's, was in the presidential office when the third message arrived. The President asked Franklin, "What shall I do with this man Zerbe that Nimitz keeps pestering me about?" Young Franklin said, "Don't give him a second thought. I see Jerry all the time on Guam. He lives like an officer and is treated like an officer; it wouldn't mean a thing to him to be jumped to lieutenant commander." The President took his son's advice. Zerbe and Franklin, Jr., remain friends to this day—"friends," Zerbe says, "but I've never forgiven him for what he told his father. It's what we talk about whenever we meet. Like all rich boys, Frank had no idea what the commission would have meant to me in vastly increased pay, pensions, and the like. It wasn't the rank I wanted but the emoluments. I've never been rich and all my life I've gone around with the rich and I find that they lack imagination when it comes to how anyone less rich then they are gets along. They always mean to be interested, but somehow their attention wanders."

Being of a sunny and gregarious disposition—someone has said of him that he would throw a party on a desert island if he had to do it with mirrors—Zerbe remembers much of the war as a series of agreeable social encounters. Not only Sherwood but such old friends as Gertrude Lawrence, Moss Hart, Haila Stoddard, Mary Jean Kempner (exquisitely turned out by Hattie Carnegie as a war correspondent for *Vogue*) came hopping through the South Pacific, while stationed on Guam were El Morocco regulars like Robert D. L. Gardiner, Barry Bingham, and Winthrop Rockefeller. Being officers, they were permitted to purchase hard liquor, but Zerbe, as an enlisted man, could purchase only beer. No difficulty there—among other officers on Guam were three friends of his who were Christian Scientists and therefore total abstainers, and Zerbe arranged to keep himself in gin and whiskey through them. The war was by no means all frolic; he coolly shot roll after roll of film during combat on Iwo Jima and Okinawa and saw action aboard two flattops, the *Essex* and the *Hancock*. At the express command of the Secretary of Defense, James Forrestal, he was assigned to cover the famous war correspondent Ernie Pyle, who Zerbe was surprised to learn despised the enlisted men about whom he wrote so touchingly and much preferred the company, and the liquor, to be found in the officers' clubs. Zerbe was also present and at work at the historic moment when the surrender papers were signed aboard the *Missouri*. No enlisted man can ever have mingled more gracefully with the top brass on such an occasion, not alone because he was Nimitz's personal photographer but also because he was a nephew of Lieutenant General Robert L. Eichelberger, Commanding General of the Eighth Army, General MacArthur's right-hand man, and an important figure at the surrender ceremonies. After the signing, Uncle Bob asked Nimitz if he might take Zerbe on a two weeks' holiday tour of Japan. Hardened by then to Zerbe's inveterate good fortune, Nimitz cheerfully gave permission. "We drove around in a jeep and our chauffeur was a general," Zerbe recollects, and then, as if to give his pride an infinitesimal check, the former chief photographer's mate adds, "Only an Australian general, to be sure."

At the end of the war, Zerbe was awarded a Bronze Star, and the citation accompanying it, signed by Nimitz, takes care to call attention to Zerbe's "manner" as well as to his courage and ability. It reads:

> For meritorious service in connection with operations against the enemy in the Public Information Section, Administration Division, Staff of the Commander in Chief, United States Pacific Fleet and Pacific Ocean Areas, from November 1944 to September 1945. He displayed great courage and outstanding ability as a member of a combat photo crew in covering operations against Iwo Jima and Okinawa, and the final Japanese surrender. In addition, because of his professional excellence and manner, he was assigned to cover the visits of prominent personages and attendant functions. His conduct, unremitting industry and devotion to duty were contributing factors at all times in the successful prosecution of the war against Japan and were in keeping with the highest traditions of the United States Naval Service.

Having been mustered out of the Navy, late in 1945 Zerbe again set up housekeeping and partygiving in his apartment on East Fifty-sixth Street. One of his chief interests over the next few years was the design and construction of a house in Deep River, Connecticut, close to Long Island Sound. From childhood, Zerbe had shown a marked gift for decoration and architectural design. He was especially drawn to French architecture and, inside that broad field, to pavilions. "As a schoolboy, I saw Madame Du Barry's pavilion at Louveciennes, and ever since I have been in love with her in particular and with pavilions in general. All through the war, I kept designing and redesigning a small French house for myself. I even built a model of it, which I carried around with me and reluctantly left behind with friends in San Francisco when I shipped out. While I was still in the Navy, my brother-in-law served as my agent in the purchase of a wonderful piece of land on the Connecticut River. I had spotted it years earlier when a friend of mine who had a private plane used to hedgehop me up and down the river in search of likely sites. The river takes a bend there and ships coming downstream would seem to be heading straight up onto my property. By the time I was ready to build, costs had risen so high—high for those days! chicken feed now—that I had to keep reducing the scale of the house. In the end, I found myself building what I had perhaps always wanted in my heart: a one-story white brick pavilion, octagon-shaped, with two tiny wings, *very*

French. I called it Windsong. Many replicas of it have been built over the years by friends of mine, in Florida and the Caribbean. For my floors, I used some beautiful old parquet given to me by Vincent Astor, who was pulling down a family house in Rhinebeck. I also bought a couple of hundred dollars' worth of fine French paneling from the wrecker who was knocking down the Vanderbilt mansion, at 640 Fifth Avenue. Mrs. Corliss Sullivan gave me some carved wooden garlands that are either by Grinling Gibbons or in his style and Evalyn Walsh McLean's Washington place, Friendship, provided me with a couple of lovely French stone sphinxes for my garden. Little by little, I turned my untutored patch of Connecticut woodland into a small French park, with *allées* and pleasing, weather-worn statues to close the vistas. And always there was the great river sliding past at the foot of my garden. If I say so myself, it was a charming place. I kept it for almost twenty years, until the getting back and forth from New York began to seem a nuisance. The times we had! I'd cook for as many as fifty for Sunday brunch—Joan Crawford, Joan Fontaine, Ina Claire, Bob and Millie Considine, the Basil Rathbones, the Maharanee of Kapurthala, of course dear Hedda. They came from miles around and sometimes, it seemed, they came all the way from Europe, just to have brunch at Windsong. I learned to be something of a chef. One of my dishes became quite famous—a way of cooking shad known as Shad Zerbe. I also invented a combination of baked beans, corn niblets, cheese, and spices that was much admired. Once I asked Katharine Hepburn to come up from her place at Fenwick, a few miles away, and pose for some fashion photos for me. She arrived with a picnic hamper full of food and wine for the two of us. I snapped her just as she came to the door. How beautiful she was and how beautiful she is!"

More and more as the years passed, Zerbe traveled. Wherever there were parties, there was the smiling and clicking Zerbe: Hollywood, Palm Beach, Montego Bay, Nantucket, Paris (always putting up at the Saint-James et d'Albany, where he has stayed since childhood), London, Cairo, Stockholm, Venice. Though he continued to serve as the society editor of *Town & Country*, he was interested to discover as he grew older that his camera, almost as if it had a mind of its own, began to manifest a preference for buildings over people. Few of his friends were aware of it, but he was gradually becoming a master of that most difficult specialty, architectural photography. He had an eye for the quiddity of a building, revealed in the curve of a certain attic stair, the placement of a bull's-eye window in some lofty, leafy *tourelle*, and a way of photographing ancient buildings in decay or even in ruins that was sympathetic but precise and never in the least sentimental. As he had done from youth, he went on photographing gravestones—the little, overlooked, tilted-with-age stones that one finds in country cemeteries or forgotten country gardens, with their sad, intimate messages: "Just Away," "Daddy and Mummy, Come!" His lifelong study of French pavilions led him to publish a book on them, *Les Pavillons*, to which his friend Cyril Connolly contributed an introduction. He also wrote a book called *The Art of Social Climbing*, which is dedicated "To those who have enjoyed the climb as much as I have." The dedication surprised many of his friends, who up to then had assumed that Zerbe himself had assumed that he had begun life at the very top of the social tree. Zerbe made his convictions on the matter clear:

To me a social climber is anyone who consciously tries to improve his or her social position in the community. Practically everyone is a social climber at heart. . . . "Social climber" is not necessarily a term of opprobrium. It is reasonable to want an established place in the world, and we all must start somewhere. . . . The happy members of the old guard are those who meet the challengers, and the changes they bring, with enthusiasm and encouragement.

He also made clear what he thought of the café society of which he had been one of the founding members:

The members of café society are restless, rich, and often beautiful people, who don't seem to have enough to do and are determined to amuse themselves. They make fodder for newspaper columnists by leading semipublic lives. Marriage is not very serious to them, and their flirtations, marriages, and divorces keep them in the gossip columns. They are often wellborn, sometimes talented, but usually spoiled by the large incomes they have inherited.

He took a darker view of the kind of people who were merely spectators:

Neo-café society (or what I call Nescafé) is a purely artificial category of people whose only social life is dining out night after night and going on to the night spots and staring at the café-society groups they aspire to be like. They are usually well-to-do but not as rich as their heroes and heroines, and they are more pushing and ambitious. Over a long period it's surprising how many people an aggressive person can get to speak to just by being in the ladies' room at the same time, or the men's room, for that matter. After a while, the looked-up-to person forgets that he has never met the aggressive one, and a sort of acceptance out of familiarity follows.

Zerbe made up a list of those who comprise what he calls the Smart Set; a random sampling of the list turns up such names as Mr. and Mrs. Alfred de Liagre, Jr., Charles Addams, Mrs. René Bouché, Mr. and Mrs. Douglas Fairbanks, Jr., Mrs. John Chambers Hughes, Mr. and Mrs. Winston Guest, Drew Dudley, Mr. and Mrs. Lewis Iselin, Colonel Serge Obolensky, Mr. and Mrs. William Paley, Mrs. John Barry Ryan, Mr. and Mrs. John Hay Whitney, and Mrs. William Woodward. Despite his admiration for what he calls High Society, he was able in his book to deal sharply enough with some of its most eminent figures. Mrs. Cornelius Vanderbilt, who had long dominated Society from her great house at 640 Fifth Avenue, reveled in publicity about herself and always affected to despise it; on her death she left several large trunkfuls of personal press clippings. Zerbe wrote of her:

In 1945, she moved to the more modest but still very impressive house at 1048 Fifth Avenue, where she continued giving dinners, dinners, and more dinners. In 1949, some thirty-eight thousand people were entertained there. Now, no one knows that many interesting or amusing people, but as one guest put it, "I was always grateful for so many other people, since Mrs. Vanderbilt herself had practically no conversation!"

The book is notable also for an account of the most successful social climber Zerbe had ever known—Mrs. Laura Corrigan, widow of a Cleveland millionaire. Beginning as a clerk in a hotel in French Lick, Indiana, Mrs. Corrigan, having been mocked and snubbed in Cleveland, set out to conquer Europe and did so, to the point where, in in the early thirties, she was able to write Zerbe from her apartment in the Ritz in Paris:

I have had a very hectic autumn, as I have been trying to do all my business by correspondence and get ready to go to Africa.

The Marchioness of Londonderry came to stay with me, and in spite of the fact that everybody has no money, there was a lot of entertaining for us. The Prime Minister of England was in Paris for two days, and he came both afternoons and stayed until 7:30. The King of Spain came to lunch and he stayed until six o'clock. The British Ambassador came to dinner the next night, and stayed late, so altogether we have had a lot of political discussion in my apartment lately.

I had forty-eight hours notice to have the two daughters of the King of Spain for dinner, and naturally, as everybody was engaged, I had to ask my friends to leave their previous engagements and oblige me, which seventeen of them did, and made a very nice party.

Mrs. Corrigan was celebrated for her malapropisms—she always said *"petits pois"* for *"petit point,"* and she once referred to a cathedral's magnificent "flying buttocks," but her tenacity of purpose, often in good causes, led people to admire her even at the very moment that they were laughing at her. On her deathbed, in 1948, she told an attending surgeon, "As a little girl, I dreamed of knowing all the kings and queens, and I've had my wish." Her death was little noted by the American press, but in England much was made of her, and she would have rejoiced to read the account in the London *Times* of the memorial service held for her in St. Mark's Church, North Audley Street. Among those present were the Duchess of Kent, the Duke and Duchess of Buccleuch, the Duke and Duchess of Marlborough, the Duchess of Devonshire, the Marchioness of Carisbrooke, the Marchioness Curzon of Kedleston, Marie Marchioness of Willingdon, the Earl of Rosslyn, the Earl and Countess of Abingdon, Margaret Countess of Mayo, the Countess of Munster, Viscount Castlereagh, Viscount and Viscountess Chaplin, Viscount Margesson, Lord Herbert, Lord Courtauld-Thompson, Lord Bruntisfield, Lord and Lady Balfour of Inchrye, and scores of knights and ladies. Laura Corrigan had come a long way from French Lick and perhaps an even longer way from Cleveland, and Zerbe admired her for it. She liked rolling duchesses' names on her tongue and so, to this day, does he.

Activity in Sutton Place. Freshly returned from taking pictures in Acapulco, Zerbe finds that some eighteenth-century *boiserie,* ordered in France several months earlier, has arrived in his absence. Now, tired as he is, nothing will do but that he find a place for a couple of the panels. His apartment consists of a drawing room, a library, a bedroom, two bathrooms, dining alcove, and a kitchen; one would swear that it could not be made to contain another item of furniture, no matter how small. Moreover, at first glance it would appear that every square foot of wall space had been pre-empted by innumerable paintings, drawings, mirrors, Chinese scrolls, and the like. Zerbe joyously confronts his problem. Should he shift from its prominent place on the drawing-room wall the samurai sword that the Emperor of Japan presented to Uncle Bob? Or the precious sketch by Van Dyck? Perhaps the charming oil of Madame de Pompadour, one of a series of souvenir likenesses that Louis XV commissioned Drouais to paint after Madame de Pompadour's death, for distribution among her grieving friends, could be shifted into the library, space being made for it there by putting a drawing by Dali (*"A mon ami Jérôme"*) in the hall, where a chalk drawing of Madame Du Barry now hangs and which in turn . . . But perhaps a better way can be found to reorganize his treasures. Over the mantelpiece in the drawing room hangs an oil portrait of his grandmother, begun by a great-uncle who had been a gifted artist. The great-uncle had died at twenty-seven, leaving the portrait unfinished. Years ago, Zerbe undertook to compete the portrait himself, which he did so skillfully that his hand is indetectable. (With a similar skill, he has marbleized all the steel doorframes in the apartment: a triumph of *trompe-l'œil.*) On each side of the mantelpiece on the projecting chimney breast are spaces of blank wall perhaps twelve inches wide. Zerbe's eyes light up. Surely the two panels will fit those spaces? He hurries into the hall, picks up the panels—they are a couple of feet taller than he, heavy and cumbersome—and carries them into the drawing room. A few moments of juggling and they prove a perfect fit. Zerbe vanishes into the kitchen and returns with a pair of silver sconces. "Eighteenth-century French," he says, neatly affixing them to the panels. "In gilt, fairly common. In silver, rare. Far too good for the kitchen." The chimney breast looks very handsome; the panels and the sconces might have been there framing his grandmother's portrait since his grandmother's day. The rest of the *boiserie* may take longer to dispose of advantageously, but he will manage. Zerbe mixes himself a small vodka-on-the-rocks, then seats himself on the couch facing the fireplace; his back rests against the pillow that Mrs. Astor made for him: "Why Not?" Proudly his eyes take in the astonishingly varied objects that he has brought home to Sutton Place from Thailand, Portugal, Turkey, Japan, Russia, Mexico, Okinawa, Italy, Majorca, and Hong Kong. He has mingled them together with old Zerbe pieces from Cleveland and with still older Zerbe pieces from Pennsylvania. The clutter, strange as it is, pleases. And every object has its story; for example, the little eighteenth-century painted lead clock on the tabouret in the library had been bought by Zerbe as a young man in Paris. Mrs. Michael Arlen having admired it, Zerbe gave it to her; on her death she left it to him in her will. Moreover, the clutter is reduced from time to time by an impulsive act of generosity on Zerbe's part; recently he presented a couple of eighteenth-century terra-cotta busts of Madame Du Barry to the Louvre.

Zerbe has an agreeable day to look forward to. Hermione Gingold, Celeste Cheatham, and Paulette Goddard are coming to lunch. He will give them a favorite Zerbe dish: curried chicken, with raisins and shredded coconut. For dessert he will serve a notorious Zerbe blockbuster, which consists of butter-pecan ice cream with cold mincemeat sauce. That will be something for the ladies to get their teeth into. He will be helped at lunch by Joseph Cooper, his houseman for twenty-eight years. (Joseph, too, won a Bronze Star in the South Pacific. Master and servant are fast friends.) After lunch, Zerbe will nap until it is time for him to keep an appointment to photograph the momentarily fashionable von Furstenbergs. Later, there will be a dinner party at Gloria Gurney's in honor of Desmond Guinness, newly come to New York from his castle in Ireland. Desmond is a Mitford on his mother's side and has the mad, bright-blue Mitford eyes—an amusing man, whom Zerbe has often photographed in Ireland, on the green banks of the Liffey. Toward midnight, he and Millie Considine will drop in at El Morocco. Angelo, the maître d', will have saved a favorite table for him. Though he purports to be retired, he likes to maintain a close connection with the club. The young and the rich and the beautiful remain important to him. The pleasure he takes from them must be equaled by the pleasure he gives; that is the bargain he has struck with them without their knowing it, and it is one that he is determined to keep at all costs. He pours himself a second small drink. He has been very virtuous of late—six weeks on the wagon—and his liver can stand a little darkening. He raises his glass. Happy people, happy times! Tonight he will bring along his camera, just in case.

A Novel Written by a Camera

Hollywood in the late twenties and early thirties was in its Golden Age. Although the Depression was to shake it financially for a time, as a cultural phenomenon it was the wonder of the world. Writers like West, Fitzgerald, Huxley, and Waugh saw it as a new and incalculable force in society; their mockery of it was not without awe, and Fitzgerald in particular studied the leading members of the movie colony as warily and respectfully as Stendhal had studied his careerist Parisians. Nothing in Hollywood existed on an ordinary scale or in an ordinary hue. The great stars of the day might have been so many gods and goddesses. They accepted their worshipers with equanimity, for it was simply the case that they were far above ordinary mortals in the perfection of their hair and teeth and skin and features. Their supple bodies deserved to be adored, as the nearest mirror could not fail to tell them.

The stars led lives of conspicuous splendor, which they shared with millions of people drudging in circumstances irredeemably commonplace. The means of sharing were in large part gossip columns and articles in newspapers and movie magazines, and it was a becoming irony that many stars reached Hollywood as a result of reading fictions about their predecessors in the very magazines that were then to publish gushy fictions about them. Hollywood was indeed a dream factory, and the workers themselves were among those who came to believe that the dreams they manufactured were the real thing. A few of the stars were wise managers of their small talents; still fewer—Garbo among them—were wise managers of great talents. In the Golden Age, it was hard to keep one's head, especially if that head was silly as well as pretty. Good luck gave one fame; bad luck took it away. It was only to be expected that most stars rose and blazed and then burned out, but there were other stars that rose and blazed and, though dimmed, remained in the firmament, content alike with what they had gained from Hollywood and with what they had given to the world.

Such a star was Dolores Del Rio, seen here entering her Cadillac Eight Custom town car. At the time, she was under contract to United Artists at a reputed salary of nine thousand dollars a week. Everything about this picture is worth close study, including the street name, Vallejo, painted on the curb out of camera range and reflected in the glossy body of the car. Miss Del Rio, who still makes an occasional movie, is certainly among the five or ten most beautiful actresses ever to come to Hollywood. Note that the car, matching the elegance of her hat and gloves, calls for not merely a chauffeur but also a footman—two in livery on the open-in-all-weathers front seat. Note, too, the suspenders on the boy who has approached seeking her autograph. Miss Del Rio is a goddess, waited upon as befits her high station, and the boy approaches her as he ought to, with a brave diffidence.

In the thirties, the way most people went to and from Hollywood was by train; leaving New York in the evening, one arrived in Hollywood on the morning of the fourth day. To a contemporary young person, this picture, FACING PAGE, ABOVE, *of a crack express on the Union Pacific line looks as if it had been taken a hundred years ago, instead of less than forty.* BELOW, *the chastely handsome Greek Revival mansion of Jack Warner in Beverly Hills, and,* AT RIGHT, *the robust master of the house, telephoning from the water cooler.*

ON THIS PAGE, ABOVE, *Falcon's Lair, the romantic house once occupied by Rudolph Valentino and reported in movie magazines of the period to be occupied by his ghost, who disliked tenants.* BELOW, *a movie set of a small French château, rotting away in a field without even so much as an irritated ghost to do it honor.*

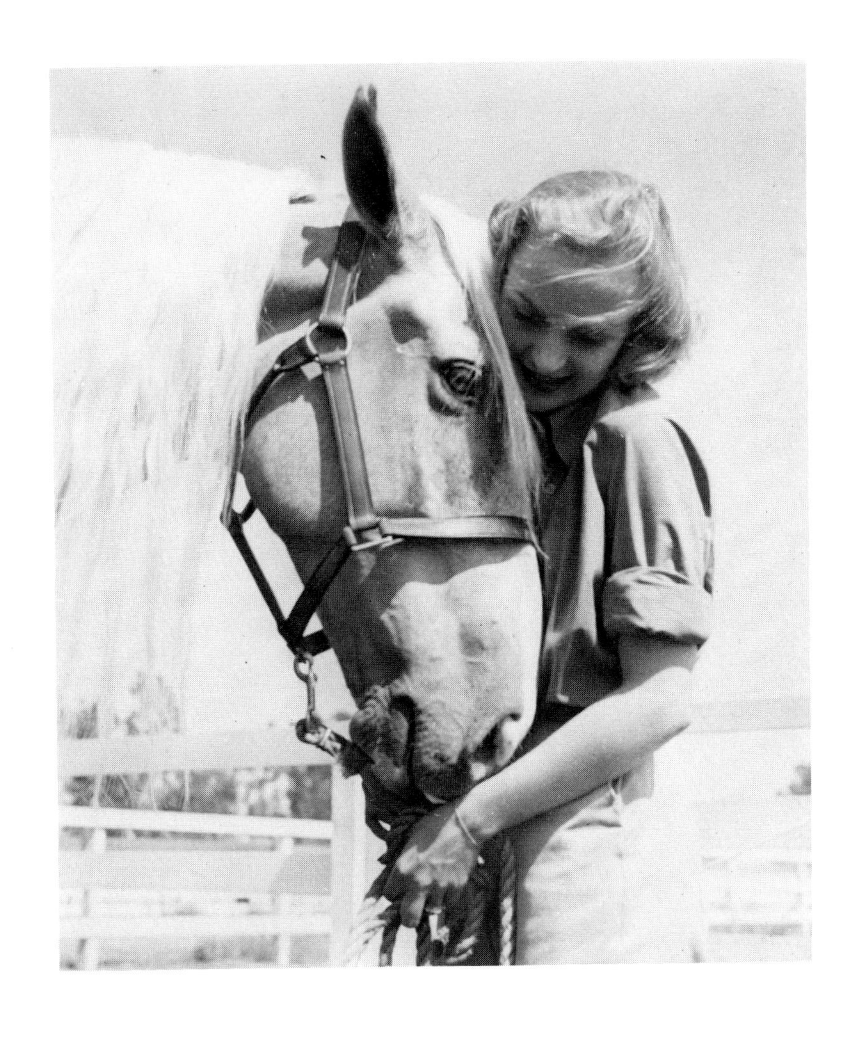

ON THE FACING PAGE, *Jean Harlow on the M-G-M lot.* ON THIS PAGE, *Carole Lombard enjoying a day off at a ranch in the San Fernando Valley; Paulette Goddard lighting up at the Beverly Hills Tennis Club; and Randolph Scott arriving for a party at Zerbe's Hollywood apartment.*

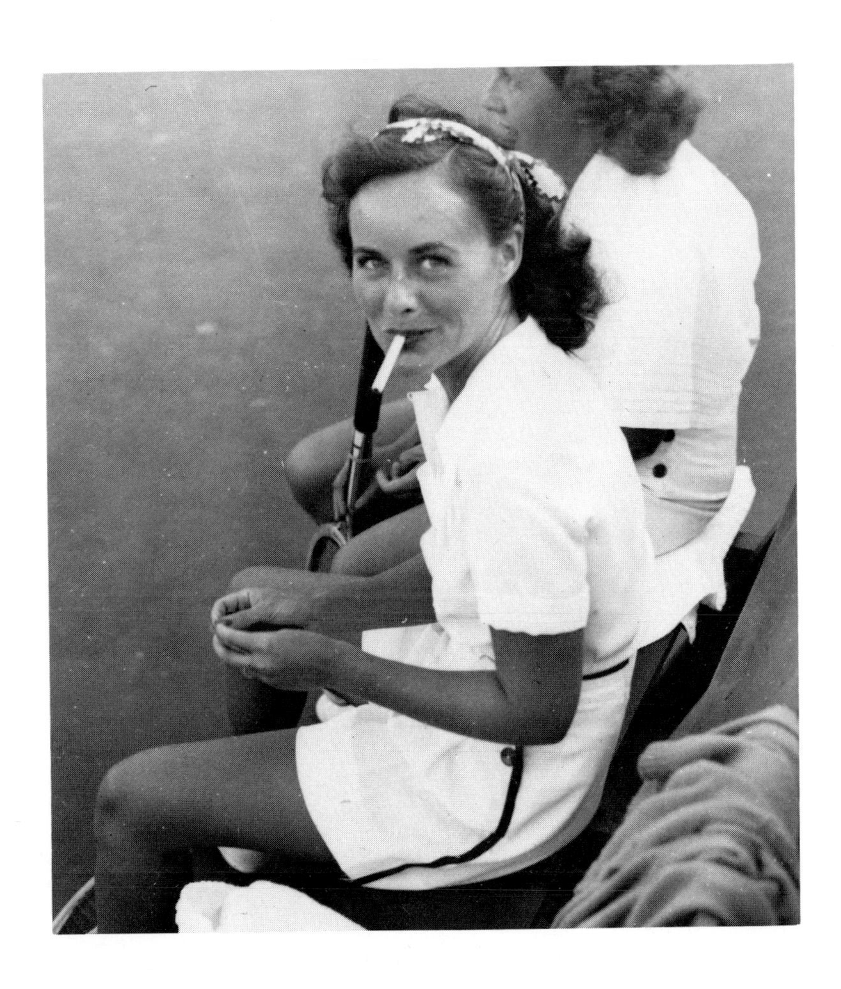

STAGE DEPT
CIGAR
50 BEAUTIES
STAGE DEPT
76

ON THE FACING PAGE, ABOVE, *Ann Harding, Henry Halliday, and Gary Cooper being placed in position for a scene in* Peter Ibbetson. *The sets in this period of Hollywood prosperity were incomparably lavish.* BELOW, *a set on the Paramount lot, representing a Harlem street scene. The Spanish-looking building to the right of the picture, with its tiled roof and wooden balcony, would be kept out of camera range.*

ON THIS PAGE, *two early portraits by Zerbe in a serious mood: Ethel Barrymore, and W. S. Van Dyke, who directed* White Shadows in the South Seas, Trader Horn, The Thin Man, Rage in Heaven, *and many other pictures.*

ON THE FACING PAGE, ABOVE, *Freddie Bartholomew, a prominent child star of the thirties. His best-known roles were in* David Copperfield, Captains Courageous, Little Lord Fauntleroy, *and* Kidnapped. *The fate of child stars is to grow up, lose their winsomeness, and become unexceptional adults. Some find this transition easier than others; Bartholomew is now a contented homeowner somewhere in the green depths of New Jersey.*

BELOW, *the singing star Dick Powell and the comedienne Louise Fazenda going through Miss Fazenda's pocketbook, presumably in search not of money but of matches.*

ON THIS PAGE, ABOVE, *Henry Fonda and Margaret Hamilton dressed for their roles in* Way Down East. *Fonda's feet are formidable.* BELOW, *Irene Dunne. Zerbe has had a lifelong interest in getting multiple images of people with the help of mirrors; dressing rooms and bathrooms have been among his favorite settings.*

AT RIGHT, *Gladys Swarthout's wig, on a mannequin that, though featureless, amounts to an able caricature of her.* BELOW, *four stars in extreme undress: tailor's dummies of, from left to right, Dietrich, Garbo, and Helen Hayes; the napping dummy is Lily Pons.*

OPPOSITE PAGE, ABOVE, *Alice Faye on the set of* Every Night at Eight, *and,* BELOW, *extras waiting exhausted on the set for still another take.*

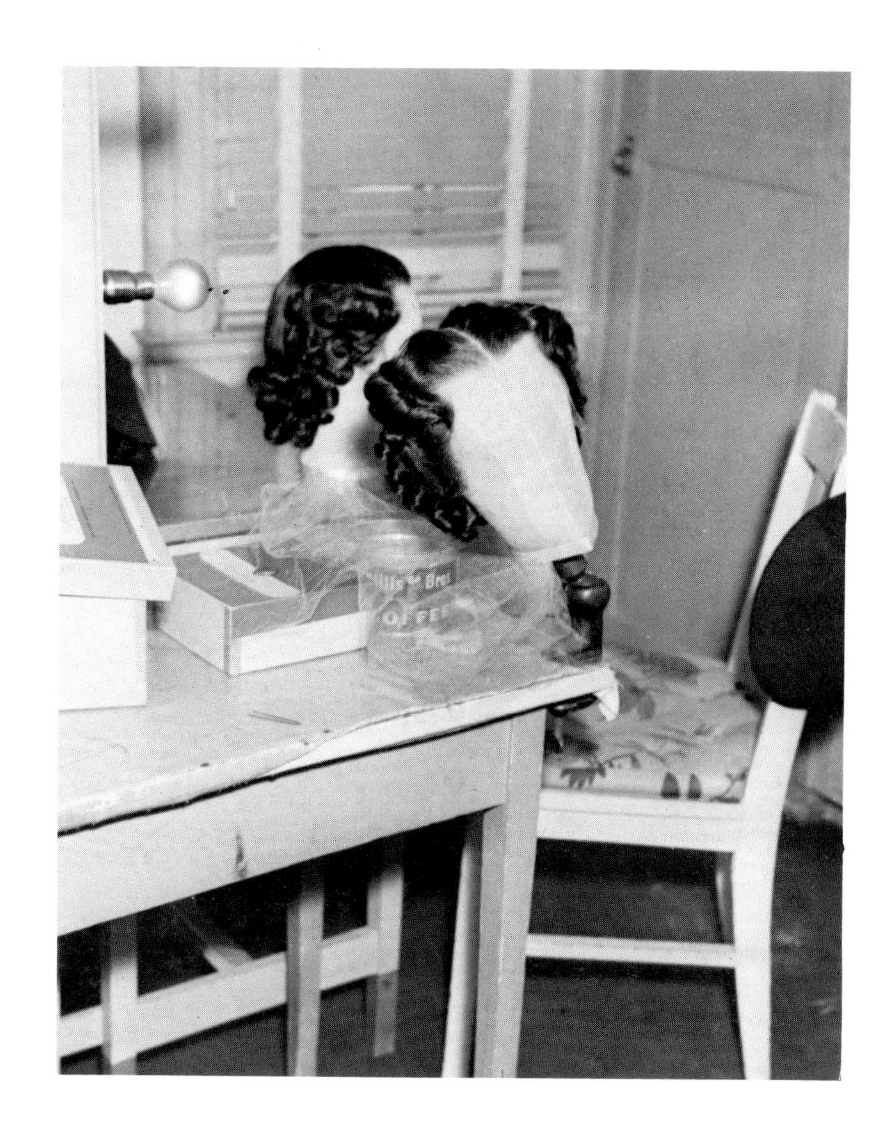

Cary Grant at Santa Monica. The girl in the picture is Betty Furness, with whom, for the sake of movie magazines and other sources of publicity, Grant was supposed to be having an impassioned romance. In the thirties, studios arranged these matters as they saw fit, and the actors and actresses concerned were not expected to mind, or not very much.

To Jerry,
modestly.
Cary.

Over the years, Zerbe has taken many hundreds of pictures of people in bathrooms. For him, the setting seems to embody the same intimate aspect of domestic life that French artists of the eighteenth century delighted to convey in their innumerable engravings of "La Toilette." *Some of Zerbe's bathroom pictures are conventional, like the one* ABOVE *of John Garfield shaving; others are mysterious, like the one* AT RIGHT, *which shows Steve Reeves, once the muscleman "Mr. World" and later the star of such Italian-made movies as* Goliath and the Barbarians *and* Hercules Unchained, *soaping up without taking the trouble to undress completely.* ON THE FACING PAGE, ABOVE, *the tennis player Frank Shields showering after a hard match, and,* BELOW, *Tyrone Power anointing himself with after-shave lotion.*

Actors' dressing rooms have always been as interesting to Zerbe as bathrooms. FACING PAGE, ABOVE, *Tyrone Power making up. Then in his early twenties, he was to die of a heart attack at forty-five, in Spain, where he was making a movie called* Solomon and Sheba. BELOW, *Power at the check-out counter of the commissary at Twentieth Century-Fox. His lunch has cost him a dollar and thirty cents.* ON THIS PAGE, *the veteran actor-dancer Fred Stone, who has dined more economically than Power, and the stripper Gypsy Rose Lee. The curious object in her hair invites taking off.* BELOW, *the comedian Eddie Cantor with the screen-writer Nunnally Johnson* (The House of Rothschild, The Grapes of Wrath) *and Cecilia Ager, also a screen-writer.*

The natural enemy of dogs and children, depicted in a vehicle usually preferred by children. It is hard to believe that a man fond of drinking would also be fond of swinging, but such was the case with W. C. Fields; having had this ample swing erected in the yard behind his house, he would waft himself back and forth by the hour, contentedly nursing a hangover.

Shirley Temple at the height of her movie success. For several years she was the most popular movie star in the world. Unlike most child stars, she has remained in the public eye; she once ran for Congress in California and President Nixon gave her a post at the United Nations. Her movies amount to a litany of titles employing as often as possible the adjective "little"— Little Miss Marker, The Little Colonel, Our Little Girl, The Littlest Rebel, Poor Little Rich Girl, Little Miss Broadway, *and* The Little Princess. *When the studio was at a loss for "little's," it was content to fall back upon* Curly Top *and even* Dimples.

Bruce Cabot swimming and showering. A superb athlete, Cabot starred in a number of movies that took advantage of his physical prowess. Probably his most famous role was in King Kong. *As he grew older, he was increasingly typecast as a tough guy. He is still to be seen in occasional Westerns and on TV.*

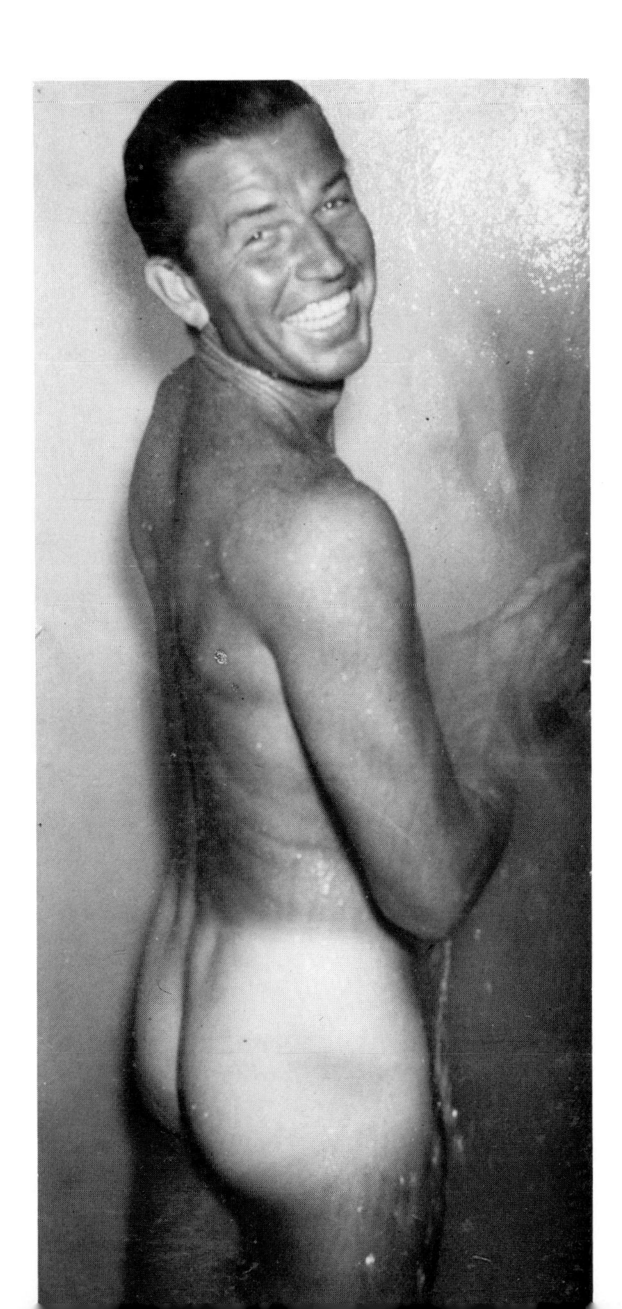

Marlene Dietrich and Zerbe have been friends for forty years. When they first met, she said to him, "Oh, what a lovely name! How did you ever happen to think of it?"

AT RIGHT, *a notable gathering at the house of Countess Dorothy di Frasso. In the usual order, the Countess, Cary Grant, Betty Furness, Claudette Colbert, Marlene Dietrich, Clifton Webb, Olive McClure, and William Haines. Men's trousers were so full that men less graceful than the dancer Webb must often have tripped over themselves as they walked. Haines, an important leading man in silent pictures, retired from moviemaking at about this time (1935) and has since been one of the most successful of Hollywood decorators.*

BELOW, *on the same occasion, Claudette Colbert, in gloves, making home movies of Marlene Dietrich and George Cukor, who had recently directed* David Copperfield *and* Sylvia Scarlett. *The surprisingly chubby-faced Miss Dietrich was then making a movie called* The Devil Is a Woman.

The Countess di Frasso had a malicious sense of humor. Once, at a party, she had recording devices attached to the undersides of benches scattered throughout the grounds shown here. She invited the same group of guests to a subsequent party and played back for them the indiscreet conversations they had carried on in the supposed privacy of a garden at night. The prank was not well received.

ON THE FACING PAGE, *Boris Karloff taking a nap in his garden. This gentle cricketer and poetry fancier was then at the height of his fame as a monster in such movies as* Frankenstein, Bride of Frankenstein, The Black Room, *and* The Walking Dead.

ON THIS PAGE, *Errol Flynn frisking with a pet and with his first wife, Lili Damita. Flynn was one of the handsomest and most energetic of Hollywood stars and one of the most self-destructive; he died old at fifty.*

TO THE RIGHT, *Ginger Rogers at a cocktail party at Dorothy Parker's.* ABOVE, *at the same party, Luise Rainer helps herself to one canapé and simultaneously reaches for another. In the background are Lew Ayres (then Ginger Rogers's husband), Joan Blondell, and Norman Foster, the star of* The Young Man of Manhattan, *in which Ginger Rogers made her movie debut.*

ON THE FACING PAGE, *Joan Crawford buys a party hat.* BELOW, *Laura Hope Crews and Constance Collier look extremely well fed after a dinner at the home of the dress designer Adrian. The elegance of the setting is unexpectedly diminished by the telephone.*

5000
miles...
AYS THE SAME
KINS CARE
TORAGE CO.
WIDE MOVING

When Hedda Hopper moved into a new house, her close friend Zerbe was on hand to record her saying good-bye to her old neighbors, carrying a birdcage and some precious hats out to the moving van, watching as the Chinese movie star Anna May Wong lights firecrackers for good luck outside the new house, and being carried over the threshold by Cary Grant.

Again at the new house, Cary Grant carrying a shaky castle of hatboxes from the van up to Hedda's bedroom. Few women have ever made such a good thing of millinery; Hedda was to hats what Learned Hand was to jurisprudence. BELOW ON THE FACING PAGE, *Grant and Hedda in a state of happy collapse inside the frame of a bed that happens to lack mattress and springs.*

USE

At the Trocadero in Hollywood. ON THE FACING PAGE, ABOVE, *two inextinguishable self-delighters: Reginald Gardiner and Orson Welles.* ON THIS PAGE, ABOVE, *James Stewart and Clark Gable, and Gable and Constance Bennett. Gable appears to be thinking far thoughts and possibly dark ones, in spite of the company.*
ON THE FACING PAGE, BELOW, *Virginia Bruce and Spencer Tracy going over a scene in Miss Bruce's dressing room, and,* AT LEFT, *Tracy in black tie, a rare costume for him. He was a profoundly serious man, and it was like him not to smile simply because he was having his picture taken.*

ON THE FACING PAGE, *the most powerful of the Hollywood gossip columnists, Louella Parsons, telephoning in some newly acquired and no doubt juicy item as Constance Talmadge and Kathryn Carver look on. Through her husband, a prominent surgeon, she had a wide acquaintance among doctors and from them would often discover more than they had any right to let her do; on several occasions, actresses first learned that they were pregnant by reading of their condition in the Parsons column. Miss Parsons was inveterately, self-confidently illiterate. Once she ran an item to the effect that Leon Uris's novel* Armageddon *was to be made into a movie and that Kim Novak had the inside track for the title role of Arma Geddon.* BELOW, *Hedda Hopper doing a take-off of the usual glamorous studio portrait.*

ON THIS PAGE, *Sylvia Sidney, a leading star of the thirties. She was constantly being cast as a waif and she was not a waif, so Hollywood proved tiresome to her. At a recent personal appearance in New York, she said, "Paramount paid me by the tear." She is the author of a standard work on needlepoint.*

A fashionable Hollywood party. Mr. and Mrs. Basil Rathbone give a party for two pairs of newlyweds: Mr. and Mrs. Buddy Rogers and Mr. and Mrs. Gene Raymond. Rogers and Raymond were mildly successful leading men; Mrs. Rogers was—and is—Mary Pickford, once billed as "America's Sweetheart" and reputed to be one of the richest women in the country. ON THE FACING PAGE, ABOVE, *the Raymonds with Rogers.* BELOW, *Miss Pickford being greeted by the famous Irish tenor and bottleman John McCormack. Beside her is Harold Lloyd, who was every bit as rich as Miss Pickford and as parsimonious as Scrooge. Beside him is Buddy Rogers.*

ON THIS PAGE, ABOVE, *Paul Muni and Anita Louise with a friend.* BELOW, *the clutter of extinct flashbulbs that remained when the party was over. A cameraman carried far more equipment in those days than he does now, and it was bulkier and less reliable.*

Zerbe's New York in the thirties was a pleasant place of nightclubs and restaurants and bars and theatres and penthouse apartments, with spectacular views. (The skyscraper topped by a crown of fire is the General Electric Building; to its left looms the then brand-new Waldorf-Astoria.)

The country at large was slowly emerging from a depression and would soon be engaged in a great war, but New York was the carnival city to which people came in order to forget their troubles and have a good time, and Zerbe and his friends saw to it that the carnival was as merry as possible. The Rainbow Room, El Morocco, "21," the Plaza, the Colony—forty years later, most of the fashionable names and places survive, though in some cases in new incarnations. The once celebrated Stork Club is gone and so is a place less famous—the Monte Carlo, whose so-called beach bar is shown ABOVE. *The girl is a pretty one by the standards of any time; her fat companion has no doubt long since slipped away to gourmands' heaven.*

Zerbe at work in his apartment on East Fifty-sixth Street. BELOW, *Mrs. Cornelius Vanderbilt emerging from a shop across the street from Zerbe's apartment. Like most very rich people of the time, Mrs. Vanderbilt believed in keeping possessions until they rotted away. This elderly Rolls had many years of valuable service ahead of it, and so did the elderly putteed chauffeur.*

ON THIS PAGE, ABOVE, *Dali's first exhibition in America. It created a sensation, thanks less to Dali's works than to his incomparable self-serving showmanship. The model with a head all roses was one of Dali's surrealist pranks, calculated to produce the maximum amount of publicity, and it did. Note the commodious Yellow Cab of the period; one stepped up into the interior instead of down.* BELOW, *the popular aviatrix Amelia Earhart, who vanished without a trace in 1937, and a convivial journalist of the period, Heywood Broun. He was once described as looking like an unmade bed, but here he appears comparatively well turned out. The drinking companion on Broun's right is Burgess Meredith; the drinking companion on Broun's left has either toppled to the floor or is extremely short.*

The society columnist Cholly Knickerbocker being served breakfast in the style to which, after an impoverished and mysterious start in Philadelphia, he quickly accustomed himself in New York. His real name was Maury Paul, and in person he was a raspy little popinjay, but under his pen name, in syndicated columns that as many as five million people were said to have been avid readers of, he invented a world of society that satisfied the dreams not alone of shopgirls and other outsiders but of Society itself. Wellborn people who would not have hired a Maury Paul to empty their dustbins were grateful for a favorable mention by him and lived in fear of an unfavorable one. He did not hesitate to make up malicious lies about his supposed adversaries in the Social Register, many of whom he had never met. He fancied himself an exquisite dresser, but since he was short and fat and coarse-looking, the effect was not always what he intended. A lifelong bachelor, he died during the Second World War and was given what amounted to a state funeral at St. Bartholomew's. Hearst, for whom Paul had worked throughout his career, thought for a while of making Zerbe Paul's successor. It would have been a poor choice; Zerbe lacked Paul's acerbity and had no stomach for creating profitable feuds.

Another successful newspaper columnist, Lucius Beebe, of the New York Herald Tribune. *Unlike Maury Paul, Beebe had impeccable social credentials, running back through the centuries in New England, and there was no mystery about his early life—he was expelled from two or three prep schools and then from Yale, in part for standing up in a box at a burlesque house in New Haven, hurling a whiskey bottle onto the stage, and shouting, "I am Professor Tweedy of the Yale Divinity School!" He graduated from Harvard in the class of '27. He was a tall, vigorous, hard-drinking bachelor, with plenty of money and a talent for English composition that went steadily downhill from his Harvard days. Beebe's column was called "This New York," and it bore no more relationship to reality than did the columns by Cholly Knickerbocker and O. O. McIntyre; Wolcott Gibbs wrote that Beebe's beat consisted of three or four hundred patrons of seven or eight restaurants. Beebe was constantly being chosen as one of the ten best-dressed men of the year. He owned at least forty suits at a time, and for a weekend visit to Hollywood he would take along nine suits and seventy-two shirts. He was a close friend of Zerbe, who took care to compile a record of Beebe's sartorial magnificence. The gardenia shown in the* LOWER *photograph* ON THE FACING PAGE *was once replaced by a gardenia made entirely of diamonds, which a local jeweler hoped to sell innumerable copies of, at ten thousand dollars apiece. Despite Beebe's endorsement, the fashion failed to catch on.*

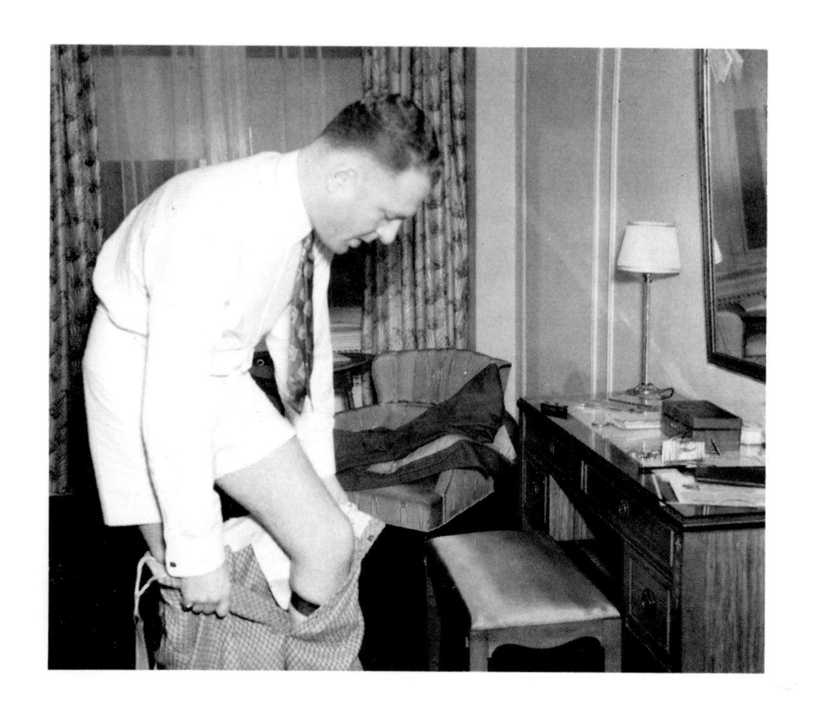

VAT
69

ON THE FACING PAGE, ABOVE, *an early view of Beebe and Paul at El Morocco. Between them, they were creating a fantasy of elegant living in New York that readers all over the country believed in and hoped some day to share.* BELOW, *Beebe and companions poking fun at a perennially successful advertising device—getting celebrities to endorse products, which Beebe himself was always willing to do. White tie and tails were then* de rigueur *for evenings out; dinner jackets would suffice for small, informal occasions.*

As he grew older, Beebe spent more and more time out West. He was an authority on trains and, with Charles Clegg, wrote a number of books about them. He lived in an old house in Virginia City, Nevada, and kept a private railroad car on a siding there, furnished in High Victorian style. ON THIS PAGE, ABOVE, *Beebe, his Rolls, and his St. Bernard, T-Bone, in Hillsborough, California, to which Beebe eventually moved and where, in 1966, he died.* BELOW, *Beebe and T-Bone at the dedication of the Buffalo Bill Memorial, at Cody, Wyoming. Beebe said that this was the best picture of him ever taken. It was how he liked to imagine he looked.*

ON THIS PAGE, ABOVE LEFT, *a summer hailstorm in Central City, Nevada, at the time of the opening of its refurbished opera house, where in boom days Adelina Patti had sung.* BELOW, *after the storm.* ABOVE RIGHT, *two ambitious classic porticoes in Gold Hill, Nevada, dating back to the eighteen-eighties. And* BELOW, RIGHT, *also in Central City, the artist Pansy Stockton, who had been declared an honorary Sioux.* ON THE FACING PAGE, *Virginia City, Nevada, to which Beebe moved; in the thirties and forties, it was still virtually a ghost town.*

Back in New York,. glimpses of the celebrities whose presence in smart places provided a living for Zerbe. His subjects were a commodity more prized by the newspapers and magazines of the period than their equivalents would be today, with the exception of those consummately public figures Jackie and Ari Onassis and that consummately public-private figure Howard Hughes. ON THE FACING PAGE, ABOVE LEFT, *Janet Gaynor and Hughes having lunch at "21." Then, as now, Hughes forbade pictures to be taken of him, and Zerbe was asked to leave the restaurant as a result of outwitting this interdiction.* ABOVE RIGHT, *Hughes chatting with John Perona at El Morocco.* BELOW, *the popular English actor Leslie Howard astonishing a companion at El Morocco.* ON THIS PAGE, ABOVE, *Cole Porter opening another bottle of champagne as the Duke di Verdura and Mrs. Cole Porter look on. Once described as the most beautiful woman in Europe, Mrs. Porter was not given to horseplay; the wink is rare.* AT RIGHT, *Cole and Elsa Maxwell, who was short, fat, harsh-voiced, and an unscrupulous self-promoter; she continuously cheated and betrayed her friends and, it seems, was continuously forgiven by them. The attractiveness of such people dies with them.*

PABST
B
MILWAUKEE

A typical night in New York in the thirties. AT TOP, *Gertrude Lawrence, Harold Ross, and Mrs. Ross, at what is evidently a benefit of some sort at the Lark Room in the Ritz. Ross, the founder of* The New Yorker, *was a miner's son, born in Aspen and self-educated (he was reputed to have read only one book all the way through), and he was always agreeably surprised to find himself attending fashionable parties; he pretended to prefer playing poker with newspapermen and cops, and maybe he did, but he went to the parties.* BELOW, *Michael Farmer and Tallulah Bankhead gossiping at El Morocco as Tallulah's other companion, the Duke di Verdura, turns to converse with a woman who has perhaps lost interest in her table.* AT BOTTOM, *the Fredric Marches with Mary Astor, and,* ON THE FACING PAGE, *three glimpses of El Morocco in its prime: Henry and Clare Luce looking young and handsome; Doris Duke (invariably billed as "the richest girl in the world") making funny faces at Zerbe; and a man wholly unknown to history, whom Zerbe snapped because of the peculiar location of his necktie.*

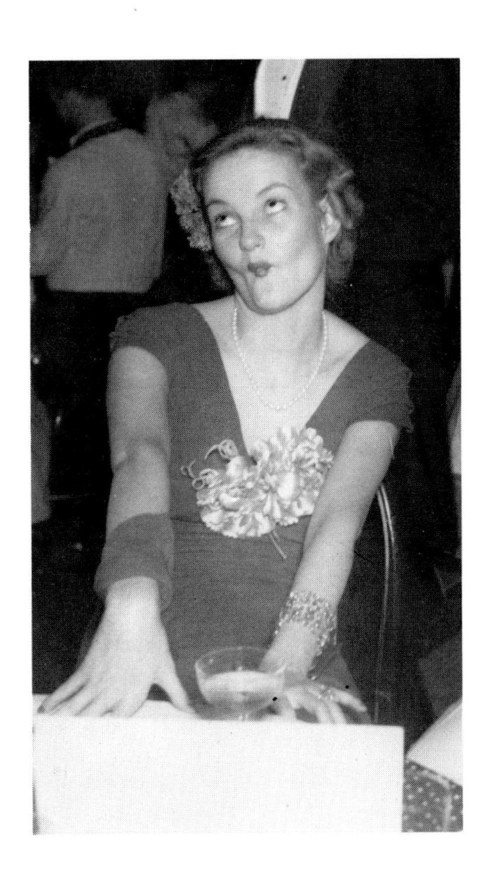

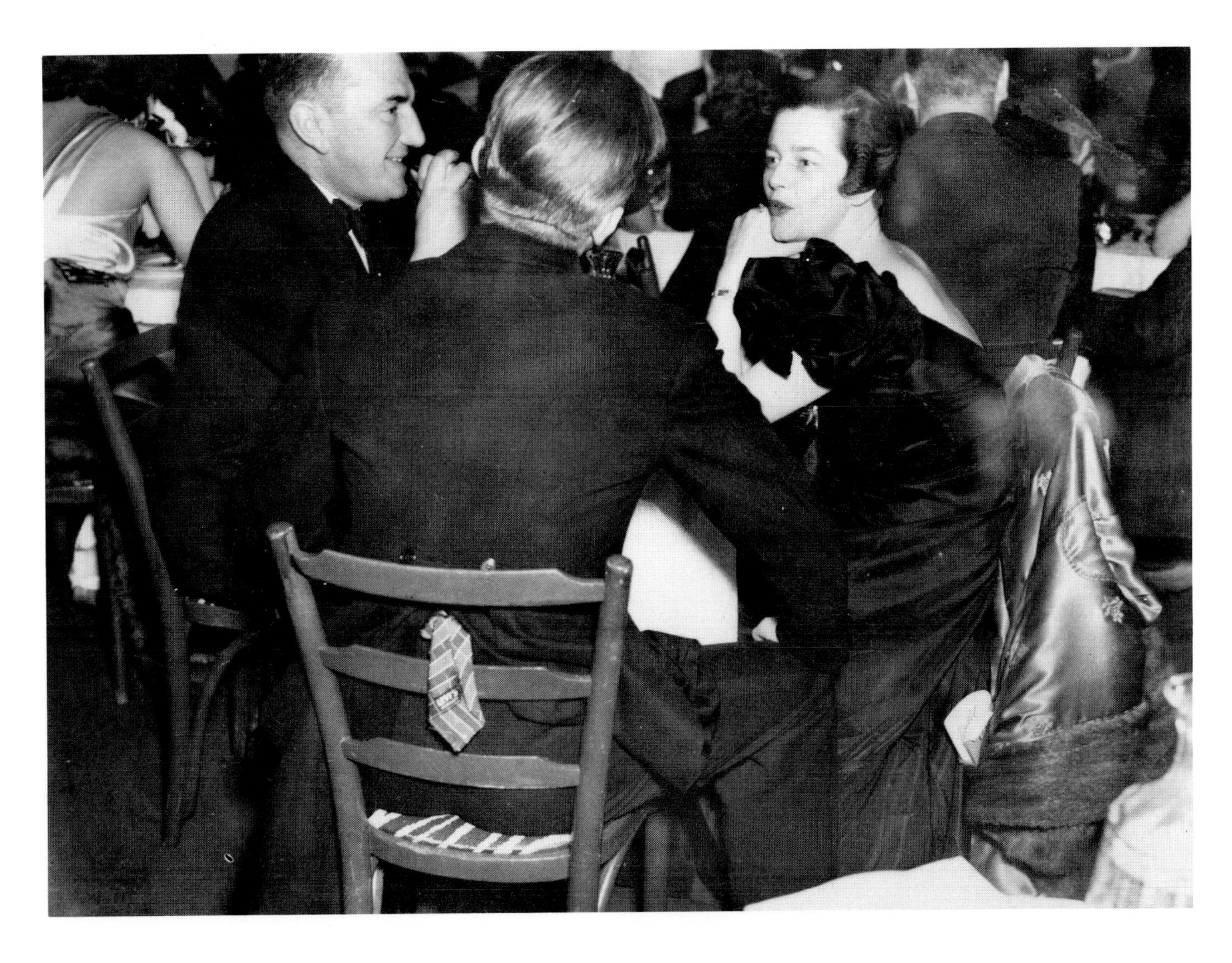

Zerbe was almost as busy in and around theatres as he was in nightclubs and at parties. ON THIS PAGE, ABOVE, *Brian Aherne and Katharine Cornell in a somber production of* Antigone. BELOW, *the drama critic Richard Watts and his mother at the opening of a Cole Porter musical. Watts was famous among critics in those days for never dressing up to attend the theatre; nowadays, he would be famous among critics if he* did *dress up.* ON THE FACING PAGE, ABOVE, *Al Jolson at an opening. Jolson was among the most successful and least lovable entertainers on Broadway; no compliment was big enough to satisfy his ego, though many lackeys did their best to devise outrageous superlatives.* BELOW, *the artist Alajalov, the sculptor Noguchi, and a pretty companion set off for Hartford to attend the opening of the Virgil Thomson–Gertrude Stein opera,* Four Saints in Three Acts. *They made the drive in Buckminster Fuller's revolutionary Dymaxion car, which was so far ahead of its time that nobody ever caught up with it. Since it had no rear windows, the driver had to depend on mirrors to see what was happening on the highway behind him.*

One of the most delightful men in New York in his day was Robert Benchley, writer, actor, and for many years drama critic of The New Yorker*. He combined sweetness of nature with an energetic determination never to let a party end; the wonder was that his constitution survived his merry abuse of it for as long as it did.* ON THE FACING PAGE, *his companion is Louise Macy, who also appears with him,* BELOW, LEFT, *as he pays off a bridge debt at "21."* BELOW, RIGHT, *with the playwright and prankster Charles MacArthur.* ABOVE, *Benchley in the crowd on an opening night and,* AT LEFT, *picking up his tickets at the box office. If the tickets cannot be located, Benchley will not be surprised; sooner or later, in a story in* The New Yorker, *he will pretend to have been totally flummoxed by the episode. He was a man who, like his colleagues Thurber and White, found himself being constantly victimized by inanimate objects.*

ABOVE, ON THE FACING PAGE, *Mr. and Mrs. James Cagney celebrating New Year's Eve at El Morocco.* BELOW, *Dorothy Lamour arranging a date from the phone booth in the club. Whenever Zerbe happened to see anyone he recognized in the booth, he snapped his picture; the result was hundreds of smiling photographs, since nearly everyone was calling someone that he or she counted on seeing in private later in the evening.*

ON THIS PAGE, ABOVE, *John Perona, owner of El Morocco, celebrating his birthday with, among others, Maury Paul and Beth Leary. Miss Leary had money, a certain social position, and little conversation, and was often to be seen on Paul's arm.* AT LEFT, *Clark Gable at El Morocco. He had worked in the Zerbe family coal mines in Cadiz, Ohio, where he was born; the friendship between him and Zerbe was based on an equal sense of relief at having got out of coal, one as a miner, the other as an heir.*

Clowning at El Morocco. ON THE FACING PAGE, ABOVE, *Mrs. S. Stanwood Menken and Roy Requa came to the club one evening from a private costume party to enjoy a nightcap. They were favorably received. No doubt their disguises would seem less amusing today than they did then.* BELOW, *Mrs. John Schiff doing the Big Apple.* ON THIS PAGE, AT LEFT, *the comedian Ed Wynn behaves on the dance floor as he thinks a comedian should. And if one comedian can be funny on a dance floor, two comedians are bound to try being twice as funny: Victor Moore and William Gaxton,* BELOW, *execute an uncertain waltz.*

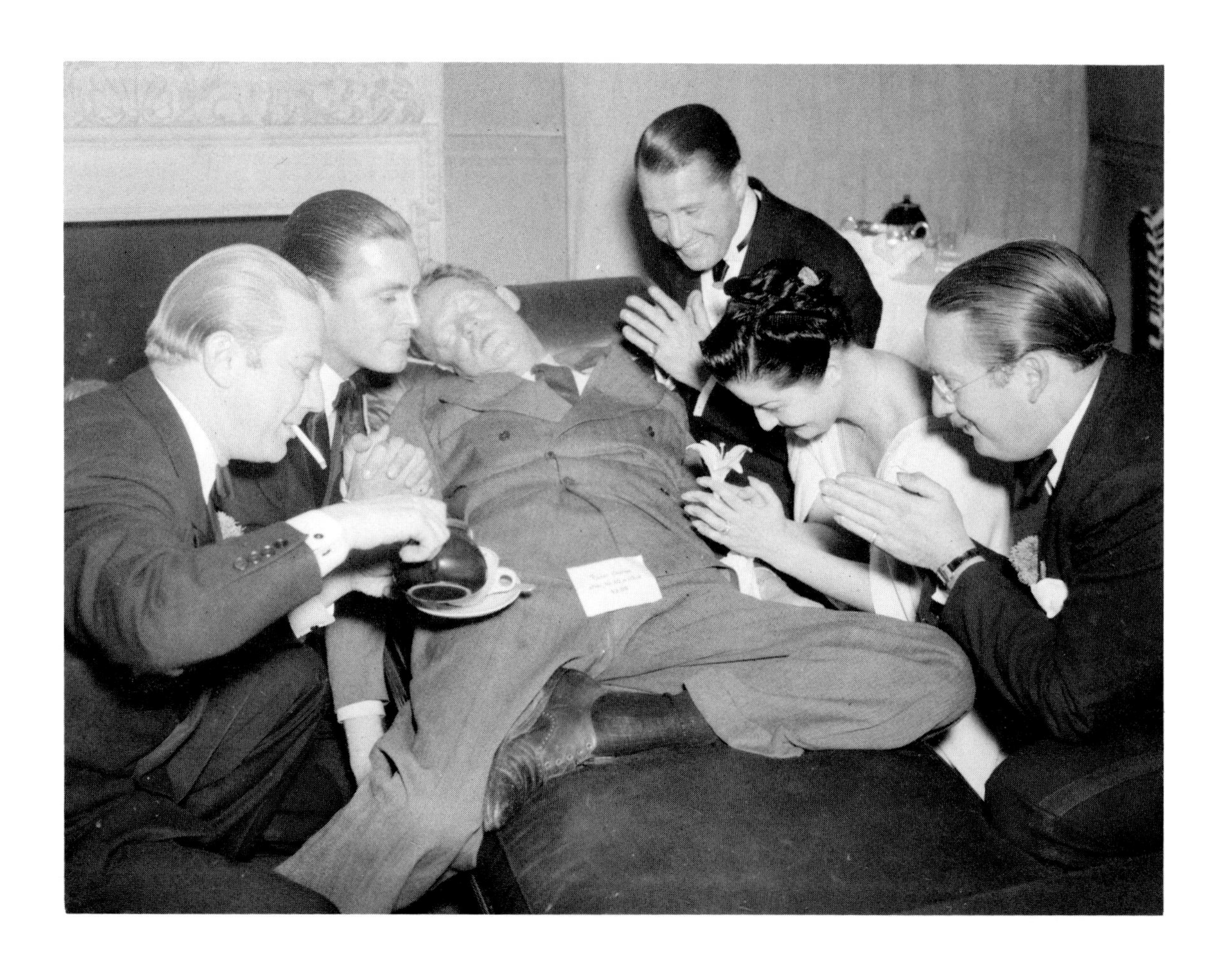

ON THE FACING PAGE, ABOVE, *a young man about town named Marshall Hemenway celebrates his birthday at El Morocco. Some of the props are mysterious.* BELOW, *another party at the club, which at first glance appears to have gone too far. No fear—the corpse will soon rise like Finnegan and the party go on.*

ABOVE, ON THIS PAGE, *Ethel Merman and Mr. and Mrs. William Gaxton, dressed as Keystone Cops, at a Sunday-night party at El Morocco, where the tradition was for actors and actresses to perform whatever antics they pleased and food and drink would be on the house.* AT LEFT, *a contented drunk. It is past four in the morning, with all the bars and nightclubs closed; as long as he doesn't tip over, he will be having pleasant dreams.*

030

Zerbe has made the acquaintance of many writers over the years. ON THE FACING PAGE, ABOVE, LEFT, *Horace McCoy, who wrote* They Shoot Horses, Don't They?, No Pockets in a Shroud, *and other novels in the Cain-Chandler tough-guy vein, and who enjoyed a much greater vogue in Europe than in the United States.* ABOVE, RIGHT, *Dorothy Parker and John McClain in New York. When their affair broke up, Miss Parker said of him, "His body went to his head."* BELOW, LEFT, *Miss Parker with her husband, Alan Campbell, attending an opening in New York. They were a couple so ill-fated that after a sensible divorce they could not resist the mistake of remarrying.* BELOW, RIGHT, *Dashiell Hammett at about the time he was writing* The Thin Man.

ABOVE, *perhaps the best picture ever taken of Thomas Wolfe. Characteristically, he has concealed his mouth, which he didn't like. His second novel,* Of Time and the River, *was just about to be published.*

The architectural historian Henry-Russell Hitchcock. Professor Hitchcock, who celebrated his seventieth birthday in 1973, was among those present at the famous opening night in Hartford of Four Saints in Three Acts. *Hitchcock's red beard in the comparatively beardless thirties drew much comment on that occasion.*

BELOW, *Gertrude Stein and Alice B. Toklas (facing camera) as they were being welcomed to the ballroom of the Ritz Tower Hotel, in New York, where Miss Stein gave a talk.* ON THE OPPOSITE PAGE, *Miss Stein in eruption. As the author of a best seller, the mischievously misnamed* The Autobiography of Alice B. Toklas, *Miss Stein was invited to give a lecture tour in America. Her conditions were that she was never to speak before more than two hundred people and was never to be paid more or less than two hundred and fifty dollars. Newspaper reporters were quick to turn her into a celebrity— a role that she found she liked and had a knack for.*

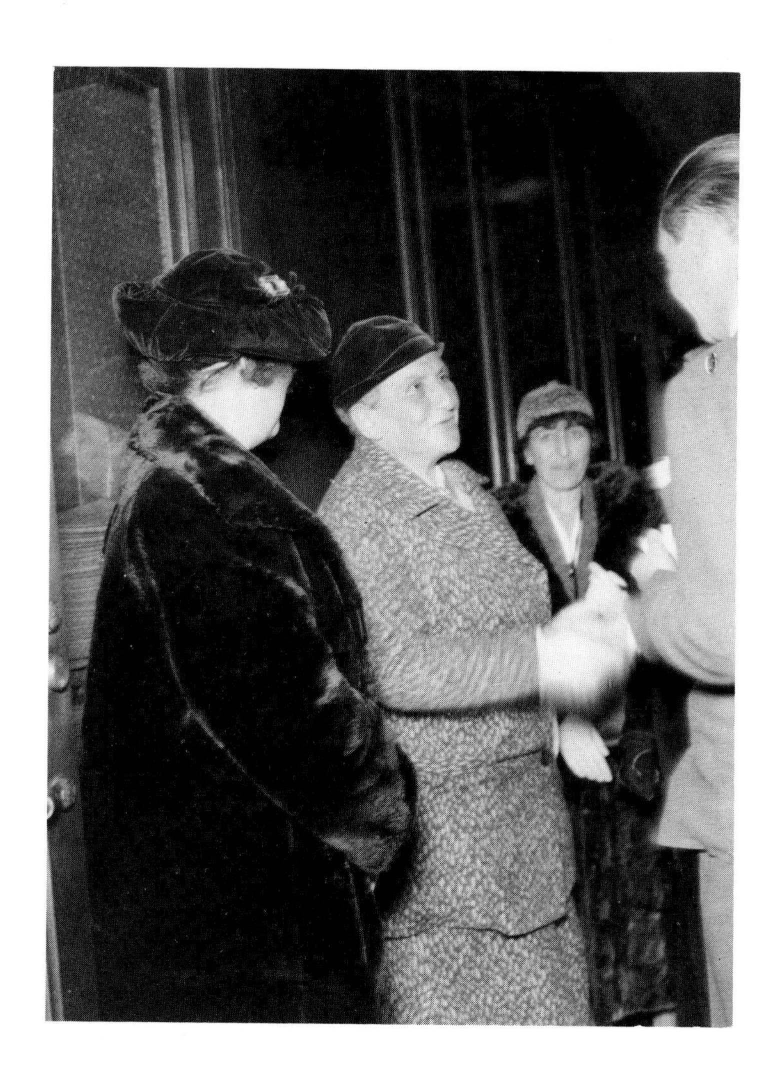

TO THE RIGHT, *a prominent figure in Society, Clara Fargo Thomas, who was also a prominent sculptor. This ambitious work in steel was later exhibited at the New York World's Fair of 1939.* ABOVE, LEFT, *high jinks on Long Island. The man pedaling into the pool is John McClain, a close friend of Jock Whitney, Robert Benchley, Donald Ogden Stewart, and other invincible merrymakers.* ABOVE, RIGHT, *the choreographer Lucinda Ballard relaxes unbuttoned in the heat of a Maryland summer.* ON THE FACING PAGE, ABOVE, *Hugh Chisholm, Jr., and Barbara ("Babe") Cushing. At the time, Miss Cushing was certainly the most beautiful girl in New York; Chisholm had the good luck to be a poet who looked like a poet.* BELOW, *Dorothy di Milhau and the dancer Paul Draper tool grandly away from the Plaza in an already ancient Bugatti.*

AT RIGHT, *Daphne Bull on a summer's day in Great Neck, and,* BELOW, LEFT, *in a* tableau vivant *at the F.D.R. Inaugural Ball held at the Waldorf-Astoria in 1937. At the time, she was the wife of Harry Bull, editor of* Town & Country, *for which Zerbe served—and continues to serve—as society editor. Born Daphne Bayne and now Daphne Shih, her beauty only heightened by time, she follows with undiminished zest her career as a harpist in nightclubs and concert halls throughout the country.*

BELOW, RIGHT, *an early photograph of Beatrice Lillie and her son Bobbie (Sir Robert Peel), later killed in action during the Second World War.* ON THE FACING PAGE, *Bea Lillie in the nineteen-fifties.*

vening with
eatrice Lillie
LESLIE BRIC
CONS
CARPENTER
IP
ES CLARE
HE PIANOS
EADIE
GÉRARD
Settin
SON ONLY

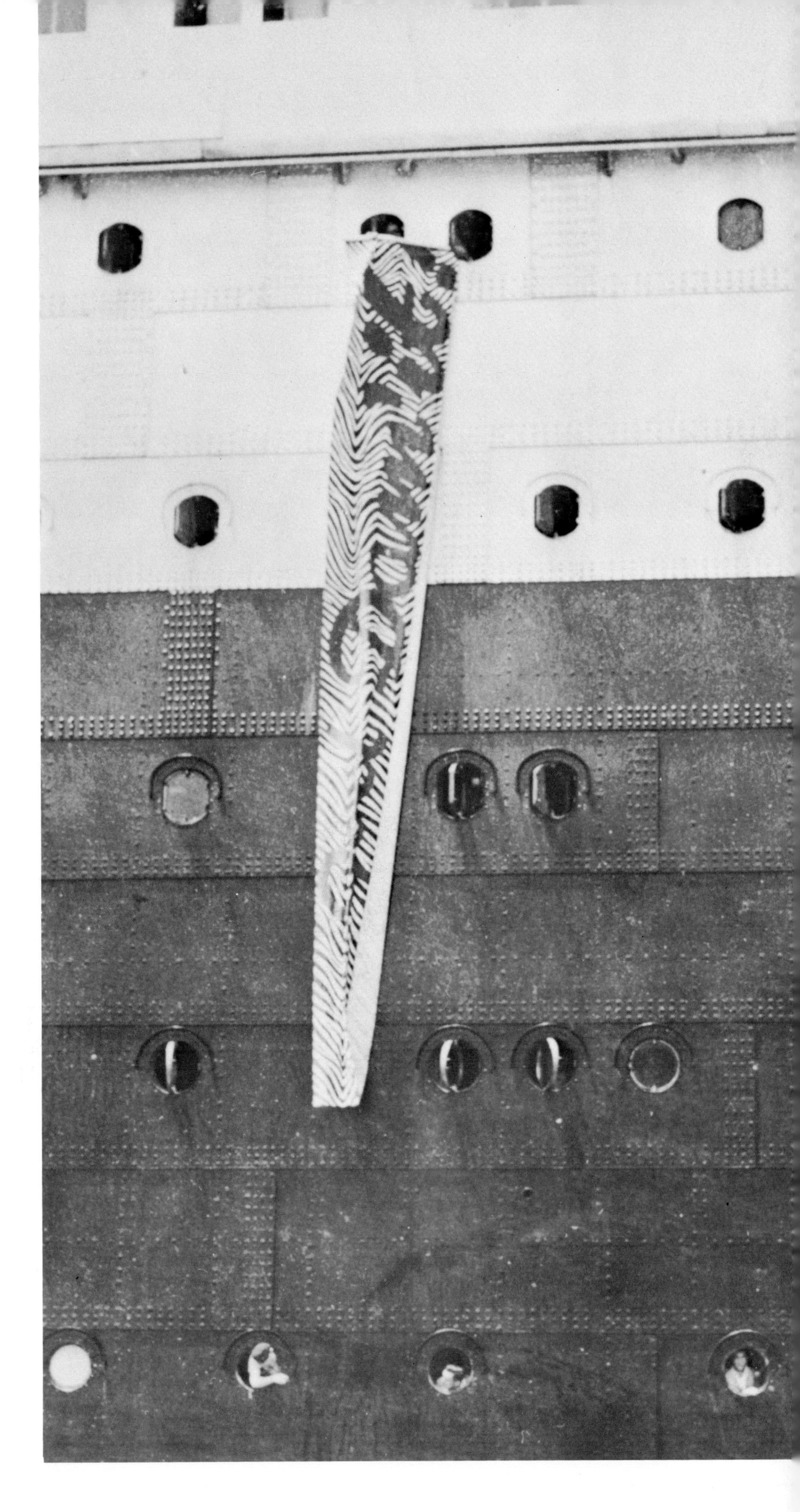

LEFT, *the opening of a fashionable shop on Madison Avenue. It was called Karinska's, and in the window on opening day stand two friends of the proprietress—Niki de Gunzburg and Natasha Paley Wilson. Zerbe can be seen smiling up at them as he takes their picture from the curb.*

RIGHT, *the tireless playboy Michael Farmer sails on the* Normandie *for Europe and indicates how reluctant he is to leave his usual comrades in the El Morocco set. Some sailors on E deck stare with a wild surmise, while on the pier much favorable comment is aroused by Farmer's refined use of the apostrophe.*

PLEASE
KEEP OFF

Brenda Diana Duff Frazier was the most celebrated debutante of all time. At eighteen, she was worth four million dollars and had expectations of a good deal more. She was small, had a pretty, doll-like face, and was civil to the press, which took her up and wrote about her incessantly. Walter Winchell invented the word "celebutante" to describe her. When, on the eve of her coming-out ball at the Ritz, she was found to be suffering from a cold, the tabloids, wrote E. J. Kahn, Jr., in a Profile of her in The New Yorker, *reported this cold "with all the gravity that might attend the last earthly hours of a dying king or queen."* ON THE FACING PAGE, *a double portrait, then Brenda and the cartoonist Peter Arno lighting up at the bar of the Brazilian Pavilion, at the World's Fair of 1939–1940, and a gag shot of Brenda somewhere on the fairgrounds.* ON THIS PAGE, *a typical monumental sculpture at the Fair.*

ON THE FACING PAGE, *a famous mishap at the Fair. One of the parachutes at the so-called Parachute Jump (not a free fall but a drop of two hundred and fifty feet on guy wires) got jammed and a young couple spent five miserable hours at a height of over a hundred feet in the air, wondering whether they were going to die. Zerbe went up in an adjacent parachute and took the only photograph of them in their plight. He used a camera belonging to a newspaper photographer, who was afraid to go up and take the picture himself and who subsequently sold it to a newspaper for five hundred dollars. Zerbe got nothing except the ride and the satisfaction of talking to the couple, who, characteristically, turned out to be friends of his, the fashionable J. Cornelius Rathbornes, of Old Westbury.*

ON THIS PAGE, *a fireworks display at the Fair. Forty-five million people are estimated to have attended the Fair; it was the last enormous act of almost universal good will before the darkness of the Second World War descended.*

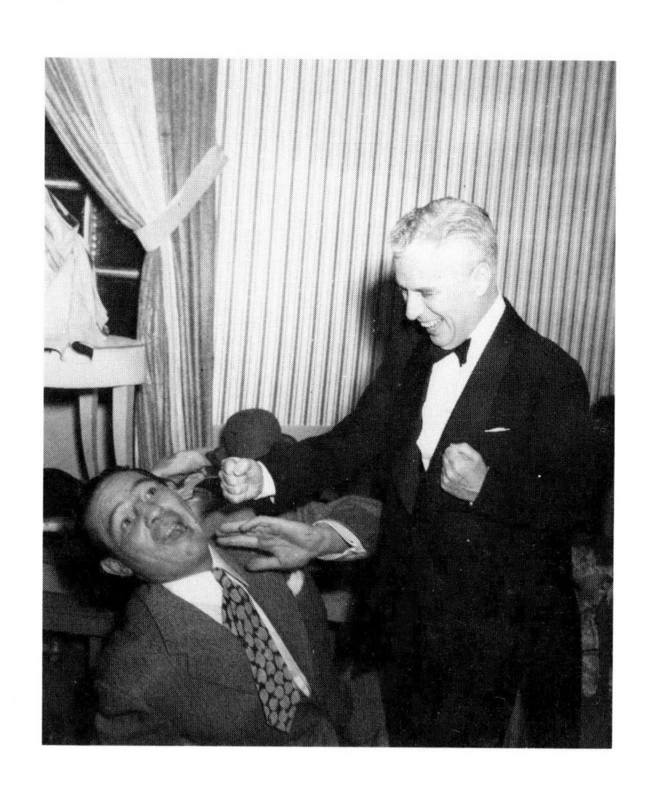

Raising money to help England at the time of the Second World War led to some curious side shows, among them Charlie Chaplin serving as an auctioneer of precious gems and—still more indirectly in aid of England—pretending, UPPER LEFT, ON THE FACING PAGE, *to knock out Max Baer, a good American heavyweight with a weakness for clowning. Chaplin's clowning was of a loftier sort, at least on camera.* UPPER RIGHT, *Gertrude Lawrence, former Mayor James J. Walker, and Richard Rodgers go over plans for the Allied Relief Ball.* ON THIS PAGE, *Miss Lawrence rehearses a group of amateurs in the dance they will do at the ball; among her chorus boys are Serge Obolensky, George Abbott, and Zerbe. Finally, the big night,* OPPOSITE. *The story is that they brought down the house, but then, that is always the story.*

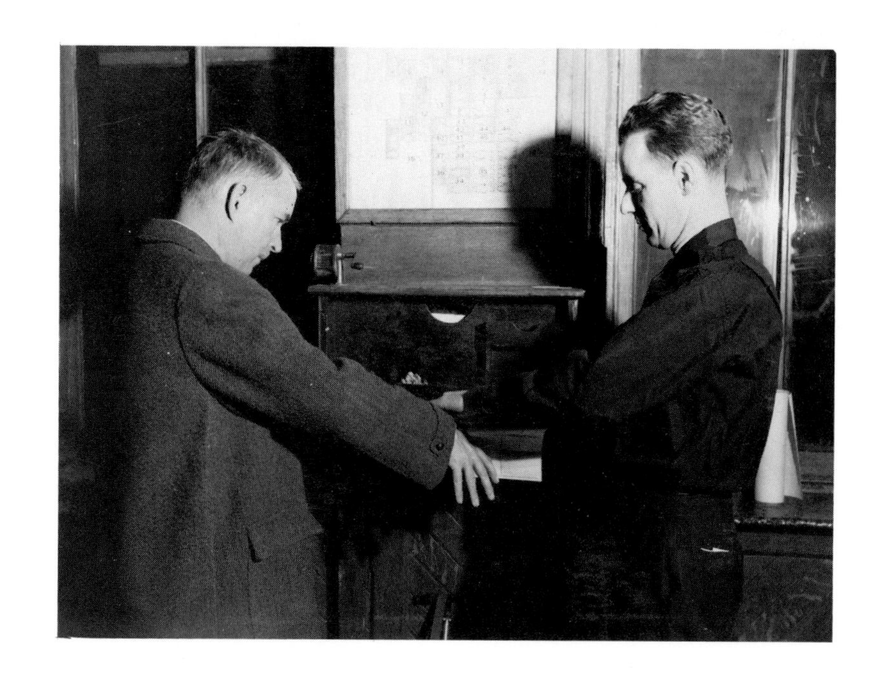

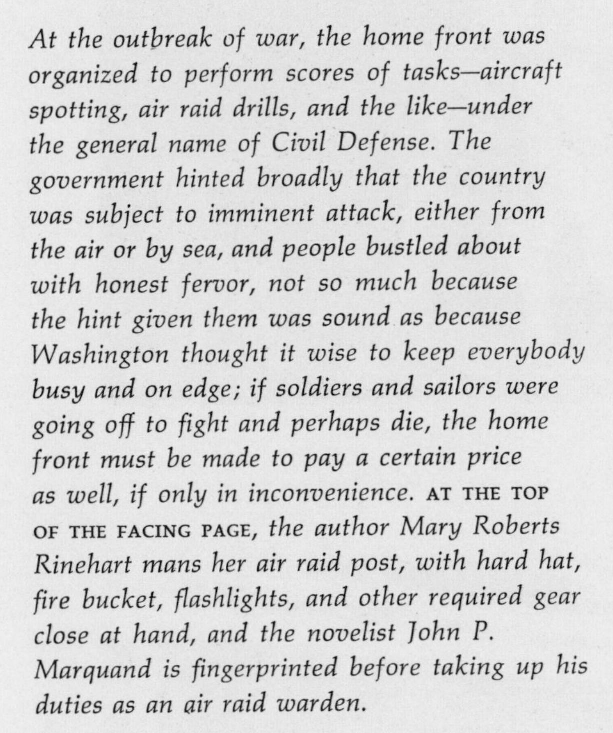

At the outbreak of war, the home front was organized to perform scores of tasks—aircraft spotting, air raid drills, and the like—under the general name of Civil Defense. The government hinted broadly that the country was subject to imminent attack, either from the air or by sea, and people bustled about with honest fervor, not so much because the hint given them was sound as because Washington thought it wise to keep everybody busy and on edge; if soldiers and sailors were going off to fight and perhaps die, the home front must be made to pay a certain price as well, if only in inconvenience. AT THE TOP OF THE FACING PAGE, *the author Mary Roberts Rinehart mans her air raid post, with hard hat, fire bucket, flashlights, and other required gear close at hand, and the novelist John P. Marquand is fingerprinted before taking up his duties as an air raid warden.*

BELOW, *the stage designer Donald Oenslager blows an air raid warden whistle to stop traffic outside his Fifth Avenue apartment in a simulated emergency blackout. Over thirty years later, in the same Fifth Avenue apartment, Mrs. Oenslager at dinner parties summons the maid with faint peepings of the same whistle.*

Zerbe enlisted in the Navy as a chief photographer's mate and got his basic training in Hawthorne, Nevada. ON THIS PAGE, *a wrecked car in the desert, and three sailors on horseback, a long way from the sea.*

ON THE FOLLOWING PAGES, *embarkation, and then aboard ship. Little in Zerbe's years in the restaurants, nightclubs, and private houses of Manhattan had prepared him for life in the steaming belowdecks of a troopship. Nevertheless, he went on smiling, and the evidence is that nearly everyone smiled back.*

U.S.

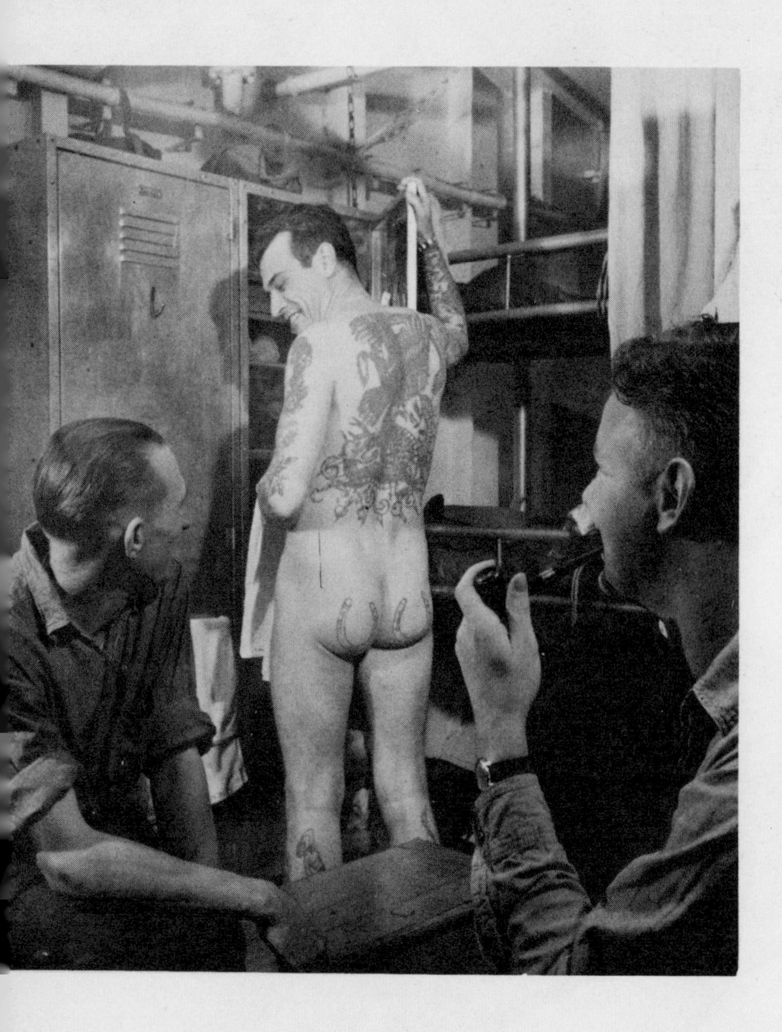

SULLIVAN, R.D. PhoM 3/c
TAXIN, W.D. PhoM 3/c
THOMPSON, H.D. PhoM 3/c
WALTERS, H.N. PhoM 3/c
WALTON, R.J. PhoM 3/c
STILL PHOTOGRAPHERS
ABRIOLA, W. PhoM 3/c
BAIN, G.M. Jr. PhoM 3/c
BADGETT, J.F. PhoM 2/c
BRANSON, J.M. PhoM 2/c
CASTNER, W.E. PhoM 3/c
CUITANOVICH, W. PhoM 3/c
DAVIS, W.R. PhoM 3/c
DEWS, R.H. PhoM 1/c
EDINGER, G.M. PhoM 3/c
EHLERS, R.C. PhoM 3/c
GATES, G.E. CPhoM
GAMBLE, E.B. PhoM 1/c
GAITHER, W.E. PhoM 2/c
GUTTOSCH, R.J. PhoM 3/c
HANSEN, L.D. PhoM 3/c
HUTCHINS, W.A. PhoM 3/c
JONES, M.S. PhoM 1/c
KOLB, L.J. PhoM 3/c
KRUSE, W.E. PhoM 1/c
McCROSSON, J.T. CAMM
McGILL, F.D. PhoM 3/c
McGUFFIN, W.D. PhoM 2/c
MULL, J.G. PhoM 2/c
NOYES, F.F. PhoM 3/c
PAWLAK, N. CPhoM
ROBERTS, N.H. S 1/c
ROBERGE, G.P. PhoM 3/c
ROGERSON, C.W. PhoM 1/c
RIEGGER, W.J. PhoM 3/c
SHEKERJIAN, H.W. PhoM 3/c
SUSOEFF, W. PhoM 1/c
ZERBE, J.B. CSp(P)

MAIL CLERK
U.S.N.

ON THE FACING PAGE, ABOVE, LEFT, *a Marine lieutenant receives his shellback initiation as his ship crosses the Equator.* ABOVE, RIGHT, *two sailors wrestling. The curious thing is that one can count five feet.* BELOW, *some with tattoos and some not.*

ABOVE, *all his life Zerbe has found his name at the bottom of every list.* BELOW, *a Navy captain with a pig tattooed on his foot. According to tradition, people bearing such tattoos will never die by drowning.*

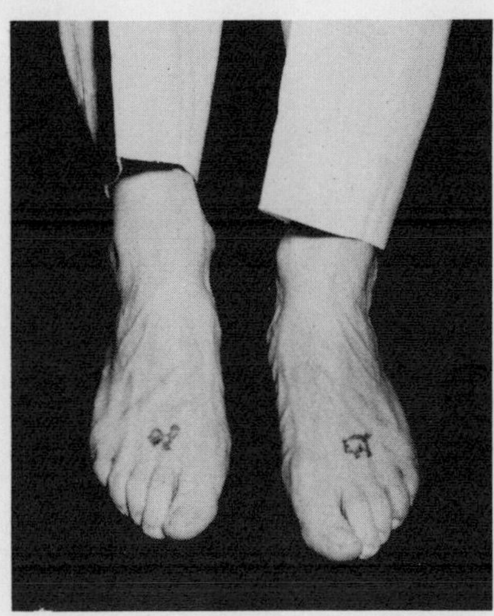

ON THE PRECEDING PAGES, *white water in the South Pacific. Zerbe served on two flattops, the* Essex *and the* Hancock.

ON THESE PAGES, *a faulty landing. The pilot of the Navy plane dies and several of the deck crew are injured. Burial at sea.*

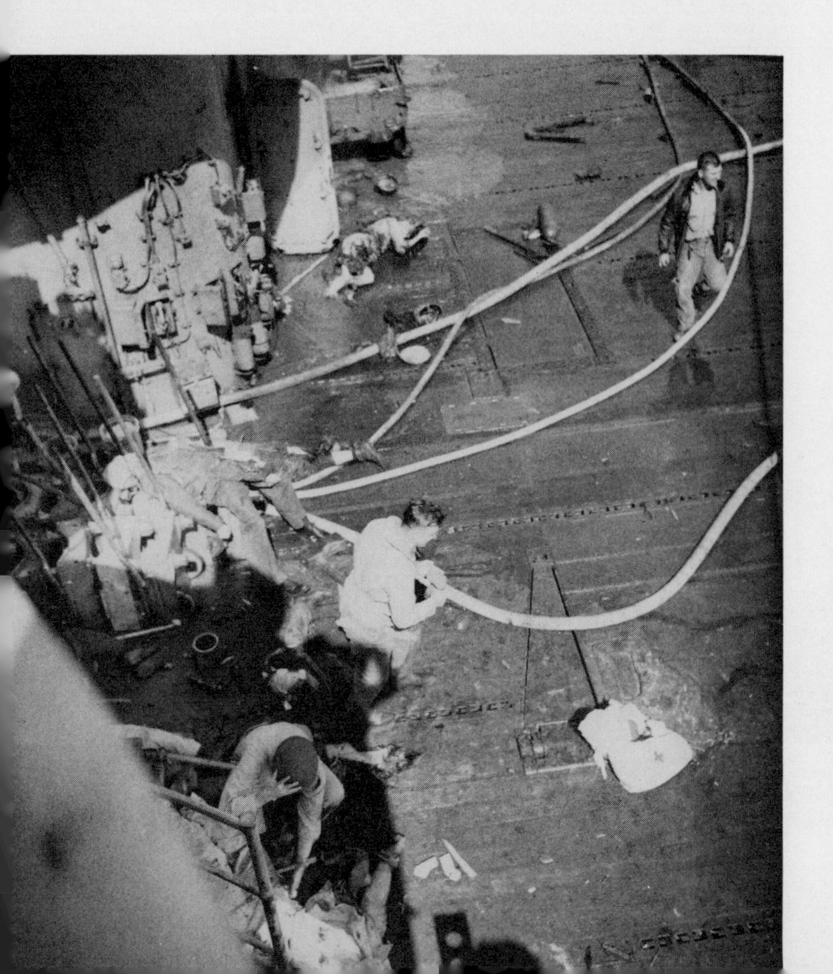

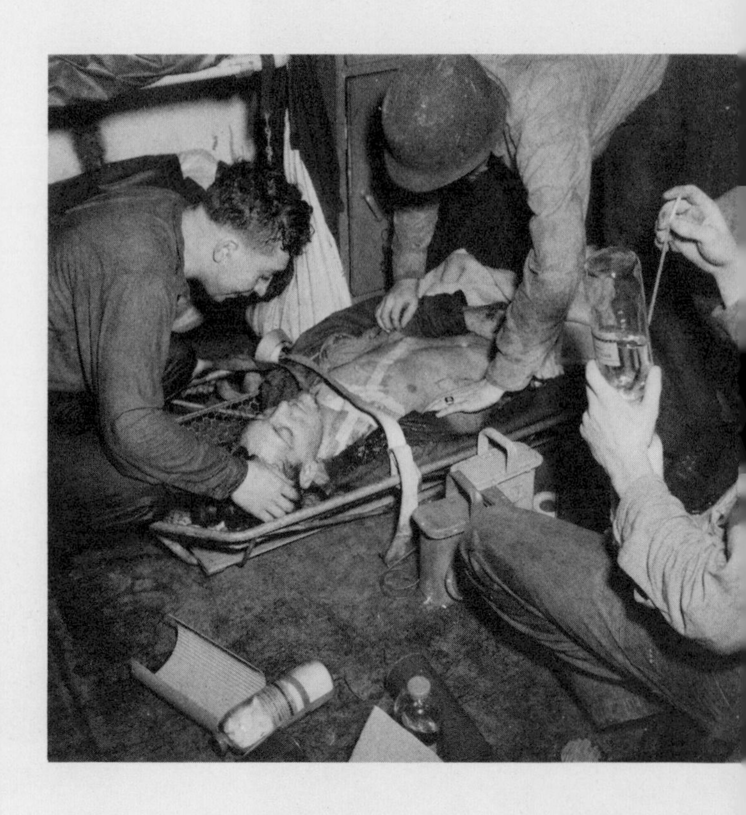

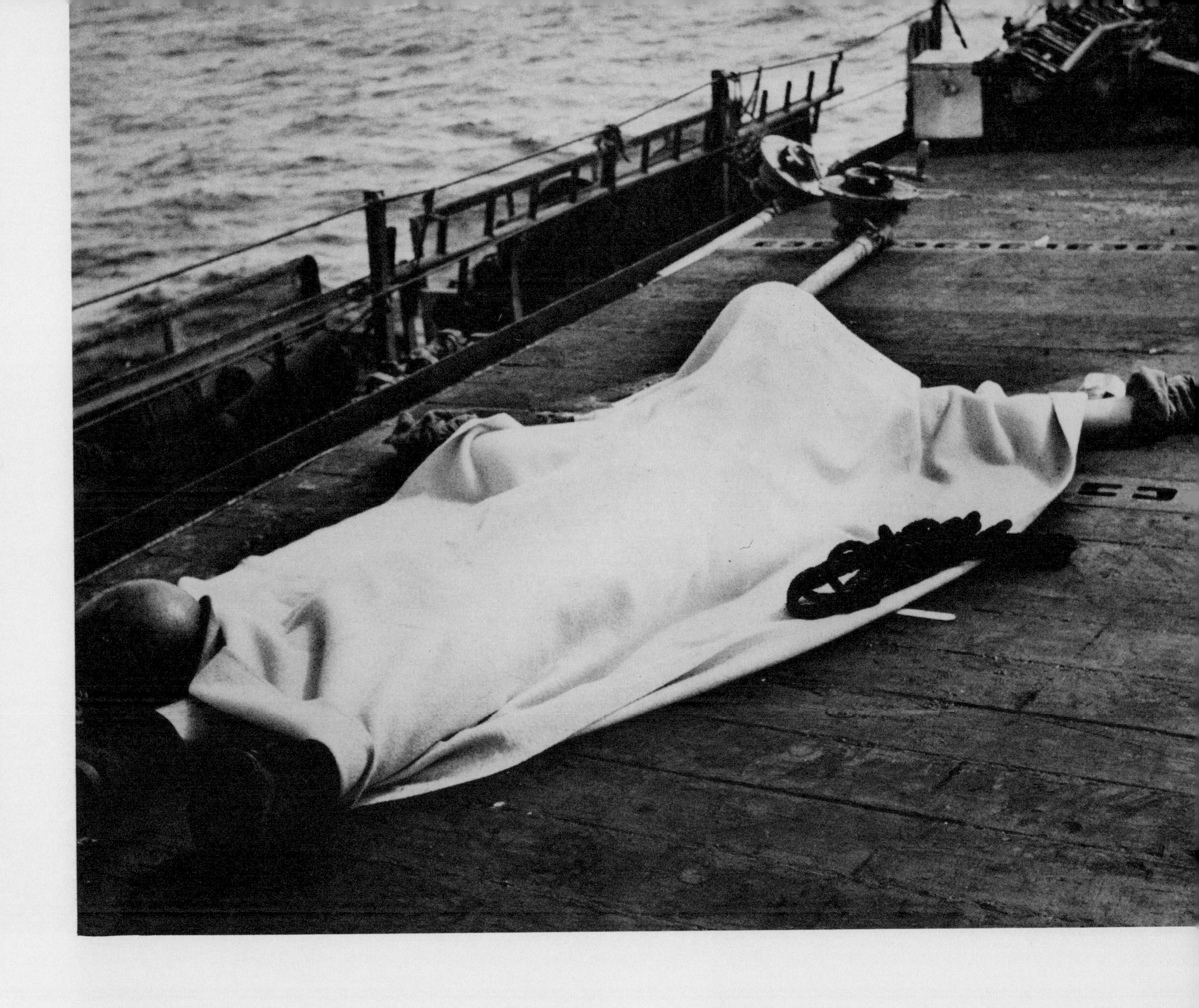

Fleet Admiral NIMITZ

ON THE FACING PAGE, ABOVE, *the former world champion heavyweight boxer Gene Tunney. Many years earlier, he had begun his career as a boxer in the Navy.* BELOW, *the perquisites of power; and,* BELOW, ON THIS PAGE, *the comforts of the perqs. Zerbe became Admiral Nimitz's personal photographer and spent much of his time at Nimitz's headquarters on Guam.* AT LEFT, *the most celebrated correspondent of the Second World War, Ernie Pyle. Though he wrote mostly about enlisted men, Pyle preferred officers and the bars in officers' clubs.*

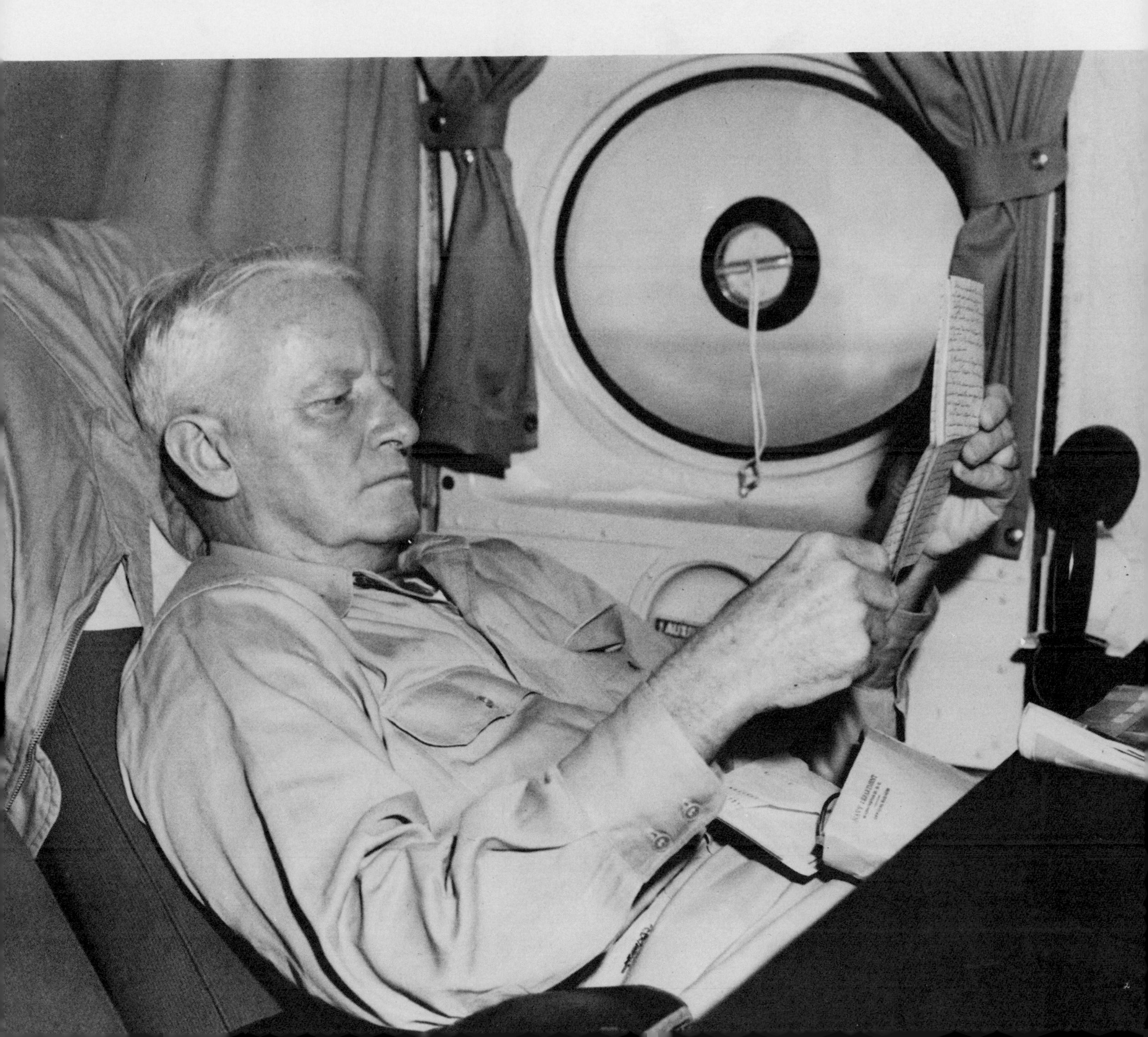

1
2

TO THE LEFT, *Admiral McCain reading a Legion of Merit citation to a sailor who cannot read it for himself.* BELOW, *gravestones on Iwo Jima.*

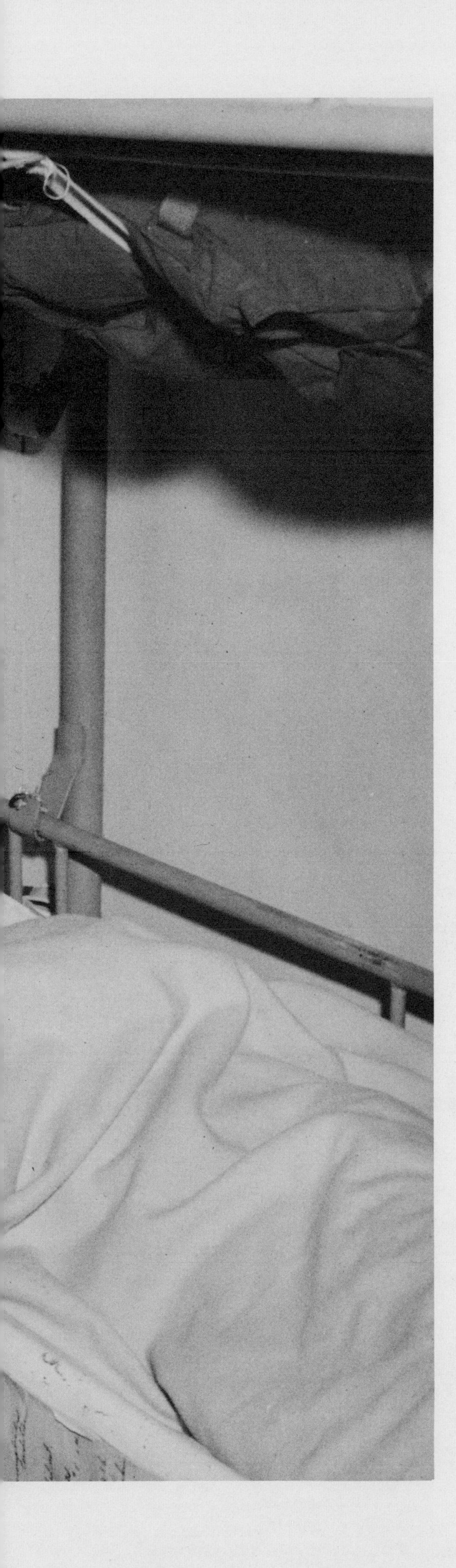

Marines cleaning out a pillbox on Okinawa.

BELOW, *the remains of plumbing at Yokohama.*

381

ON THE FACING PAGE, *a U.S. cemetery on Iwo Jima, and a child seated among rubble.* ON THIS PAGE, *a native cemetery on Guam.*

ON THE FACING PAGE, BELOW, *all that remains of a water buffalo slain for a feast on Guam. Native children ate the warm raw flesh of the newly slaughtered animal.* ABOVE, *Marines cooking chow among funerary ornaments on Okinawa.*

AT LEFT, *Lieutenant Commander Franklin D. Roosevelt, Jr.* BELOW, *Gertrude Lawrence arrives on Guam to entertain the troops. Her writing at the bottom of the picture reads, "Darling Jerry. All my love. Gee. Guam. 1945."*

Zerbe served as Admiral Nimitz's personal photographer at his headquarters on Guam. His duties included taking photographs of whatever V.I.P.'s happened to stop off at Guam, and it was often the case that they turned out to be old friends. ON THE FACING PAGE, ABOVE, *Robert E. Sherwood, playwright and speech-writer for F.D.R.* BELOW, *the playwright Moss Hart hamming it up by pretending to climb a coconut palm. Hart, Gertrude Lawrence, Haila Stoddard, and other theatrical figures journeyed through the South Pacific entertaining the troops.* ABOVE, *Gertrude Lawrence enjoying a swim.* LEFT, *Miss Stoddard and some implausible props.*

By Navy regulation, officers were allowed to date women personnel, but enlisted men were not. ABOVE, *on the beach on Guam, an officer and a nurse make love.* ON THE FACING PAGE, *an enlisted man makes do.*

The end of the war against the Japanese. The surrender papers are signed aboard the Missouri. ON THE FACING PAGE, *Lieutenant General Robert M. Eichelberger in Japan. He was General MacArthur's right-hand man and Zerbe's uncle. When the Lieutenant General took a holiday tour of Japan, he saw to it that the Chief Photographer's Mate went along with him.*

On being mustered out of the service with a Bronze Star ("for meritorious service in connection with operations against the enemy"), the Chief Photographer's Mate was delighted to return to his apartment on East Fifty-sixth Street, New York. ABOVE, *a blizzard rages on Fifth Avenue on the day after Christmas, 1947. Zerbe took the picture from high in the Saks Fifth Avenue building. Even in emergencies, his point of vantage has always tended to be a fashionable one; he had gone to Saks to exchange some Christmas presents.* ON THE FACING PAGE, *sleighs outside Zerbe's apartment. The puzzle on such occasions is where the sleighs come from: who keeps them hidden away in some corner of the crowded city, where every foot of space is valuable, for the perhaps once-in-twenty-years time that they are needed?*

New York Herald Tribune

LATE CITY EDITION

Record 25.4-Inch Snowfall Paralyzes City; Rail and Bus Failure Maroons Thousands

Major Roads Blocked by 16-Hr. Storm

Some portraits. ON THE FACING PAGE, ABOVE LEFT, *a study in black and white: Mrs. Frank Gould and her daughter Pamela Curran. If you are blonde and wear a white dress, plainly your canine accessory should be a black poodle; if you are dark haired and wear a black dress, a white poodle is called for.* AT RIGHT, *Ginger Rogers affects to receive a bouquet from an admirer at the St. Regis.* BELOW, LEFT, *Mrs. Hsueh L. Hsieh (the former Marion Saunders) with Mimi and Suzy, and,* BELOW, RIGHT, *Lady Mendl with Hilda West and Blu-Blu.*

ON THIS PAGE, *a New York custom that has vanished: the once obligatory Easter Parade on Fifth Avenue. Buildings can vanish as readily as customs in New York. In the picture on page 138, the Best & Co. building, an edge of which is seen here to the north of St. Patrick's, had not yet been built; in 1973, it had been torn down and replaced.*

ABOVE, *Adele Astaire and Harry Evans reviving the Charleston at a benefit held in the Plaza ballroom. The master of ceremonies is Serge Obolensky, who evidently wonders where his next line is coming from.* AT LEFT, *Marlene Dietrich and Clifton Webb execute a decorous two-step.* ON THE FACING PAGE, ABOVE, *Ginger Rogers and Paul Hartman greeting Ethel Merman. After more than forty years in full, brassy cry, Miss Merman is currently considering a Broadway production.* BELOW, *Michael Arlen, Hedda Hopper, and Clare Luce in smiling colloquy. The pert creature glancing Zerbeward from the next table is the famous beauty Mrs. William Rhinelander Stewart.*

Throughout his career, Zerbe had made a hobby of taking pictures of people in front of their portraits. ON THE FACING PAGE, ABOVE, *Mary Sanford sitting, and,* BELOW, *Georgia O'Keeffe before her portrait by Eugene Speicher.* ON THIS PAGE, ABOVE, *Frankie Cheney with her portrait by de Chirico; the artist himself lounges against a singularly inappropriate papier-mâché fireplace.* AT LEFT, *Ilka Chase before a portrait of her by William Draper.*

ON THIS PAGE, *Clifton Webb sits below Clifton Webb.* ON THE FACING PAGE, ABOVE, *Maud Seligman before her portrait by Tokio Payne. For over fifty years, Maud and Eustace Seligman have been indefatigable partygivers and partygoers. A hard-working Wall Street lawyer with an interest in foreign affairs, Seligman is always organizing journeys to far-off places. If the Seligmans cannot be reached at home in New York or in Greenwich, look for them in Bangkok or Nepal.* BELOW, *Mrs. Harrison Williams and one of the several portraits of her painted by Dali.*

ON THE FACING PAGE, UPPER LEFT, *Clifton Webb and Garbo looking over the spread at one of the Russian Easter parties given by Valentina, a leading dress designer of the day and close friend of Garbo.* UPPER RIGHT, *Garbo on guard—Zerbe is a friend but he is also a photographer and she will have nothing to do with photographers.* LOWER LEFT, *a conversation at Zerbe's: Gloria Swanson, Hedda Hopper, Adele Astaire Douglass, and Michael Arlen, who was surely one of the best-dressed writers that ever lived.* LOWER RIGHT, *Valentina at East Hampton, posing on the bonnet of a well-traveled Cord.* ON THIS PAGE, *Valentina and ten ducks.*

The night of the opening of A Streetcar Named Desire. ON THIS PAGE, *a youthful Tennessee Williams, looking understandably pleased, lounges beside the producer Irene Selznick, as she exchanges congratulations with Elia Kazan, who directed the play. In the role of Stanley Kowalski, a young actor named Marlon Brando made himself famous overnight. Brando, who was already a master of truculent bad manners, refused to let any photographs be taken of him, but on learning that Zerbe was a friend of Garbo, Dietrich, and other actresses whom he admired, he invited Zerbe to come next day to the shabby little apartment on West Fifty-second Street that he shared with his sister and her children and take the candid shots shown* ON THE FACING PAGE.

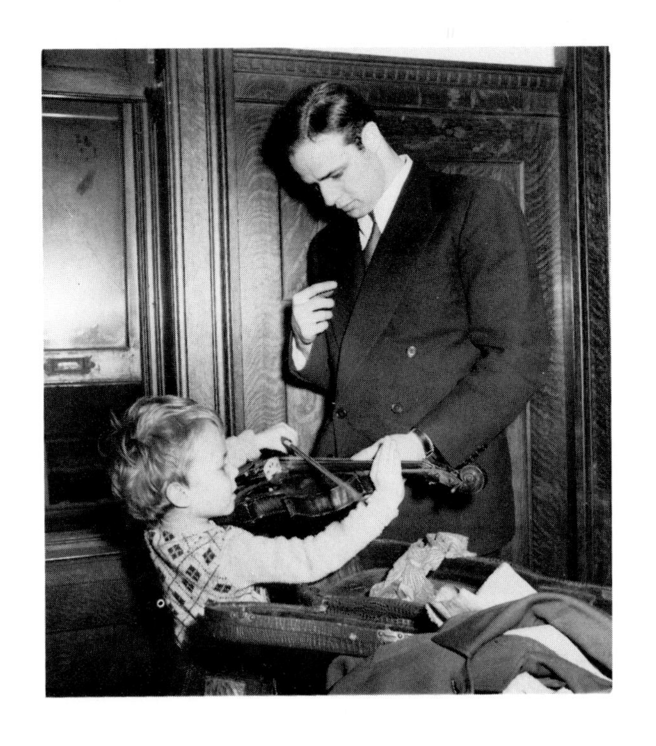

Long after the war, damage caused by the war remained visible throughout Europe. ON THE FACING PAGE, ABOVE, *the pier of a bombed-out bridge in the South of France.* BELOW, *a more welcome symbol of the postwar era: an early bikini.*

ON THIS PAGE, *a favorite playground of the rich, especially of the new rich: the plunge of the Hotel du Cap, at Cap d'Antibes. The undiscovered summertime Riviera of the Porters and Murphys may have vanished in the dust of innumerable cars and trippers, but beautiful women and handsome men have been browning themselves on these rocks since Roman times and will no doubt continue to do so.*

There are people who remain the favorite subjects for photographers year after year, decade after decade. Among such subjects are Prince Rainier, Princess Grace, Aristotle Onassis, and Maria Callas, to say nothing of Mrs. Lytle Hull, a sliver of whose visage appears at the BOTTOM OF THE FACING PAGE. *(The occasion was the luncheon announcing the engagement of Miss Kelly, of Philadelphia, to the Prince of Monaco.)* ABOVE, ON THE FACING PAGE, *are the Prince and Onassis sampling clams at the opening of a resort hotel on Majorca.* ON THIS PAGE, *Onassis, with Miss Callas, toasts Zerbe in what looks like milk but is surely ouzo.*

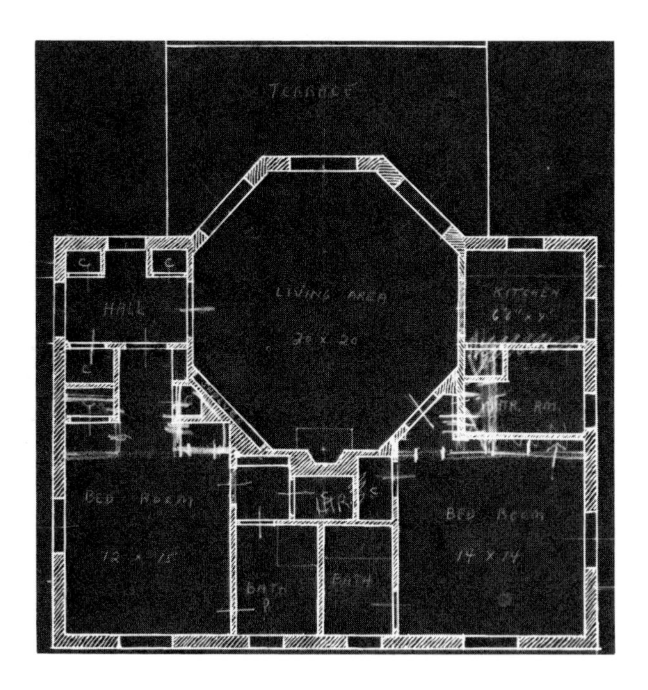

In the late nineteen-forties, Zerbe set about building a house on a few acres of choice land facing the Connecticut River, near Essex. He had been working over the plans for years; they kept getting smaller in scale as the cost of building went up. In the end, he built a small white pavilion in the French style and set about turning his Connecticut fields and woodland into a French park. He called the place Windsong. ON THE FACING PAGE, *an accident that took place near Windsong and that Zerbe remarkably survived with minor injuries. The station wagon that has so obviously left the road is his. Though in great pain, Zerbe could not resist taking a picture of the lovely view.*

BEWARE!
VICIOUS OWNER

Zerbe entertained continuously at Windsong; fifty guests for Sunday brunch was a commonplace. It was here that he invented a number of well-known and, to gourmets, perhaps scandalous dishes, including a dessert that consists of butter-pecan ice cream with a canned cold mincemeat sauce. AT LEFT, *Zerbe locking up on a Monday morning, as he sets off for New York. Windsong was found to work so well as a house that at least seven replicas of it have been built by friends of Zerbe. The one at the* BOTTOM OF THE FACING PAGE *is in Florida.*

Katharine Hepburn came to Windsong one day to pose for some fashion photographs. When Zerbe opened the door, Hepburn stood there just as he has taken her in the photograph AT THE TOP OF THE FACING PAGE. *In the hamper she had brought along a picnic lunch for the two of them.* ABOVE, ON THIS PAGE, *the allée at Windsong leading to the river. Zerbe's success in giving the landscape a Gallic gloss may be seen by comparing the upper photograph with the lower, which is of the garden at Château Beychevelle.*

When Jack and Drue Heinz gave a housewarming party at their new apartment overlooking the East River, the interior decoration turned out to be far from complete. With characteristic resourcefulness, Mrs. Heinz posted monkey marionettes of painters before the unfinished walls and had her friend Charles Addams provide temporary pictures in place of the Heinzes' own distinguished collection. ON THIS PAGE, *Drue Heinz at dawn as the happy housewarming drew to a close.* ON THE FACING PAGE, BELOW, *Ina Claire and Henry Luce kittenishly capering at Elsa Maxwell's ball at the Waldorf. Luce, who was rarely kittenish, rarely capered.*

ATLAS

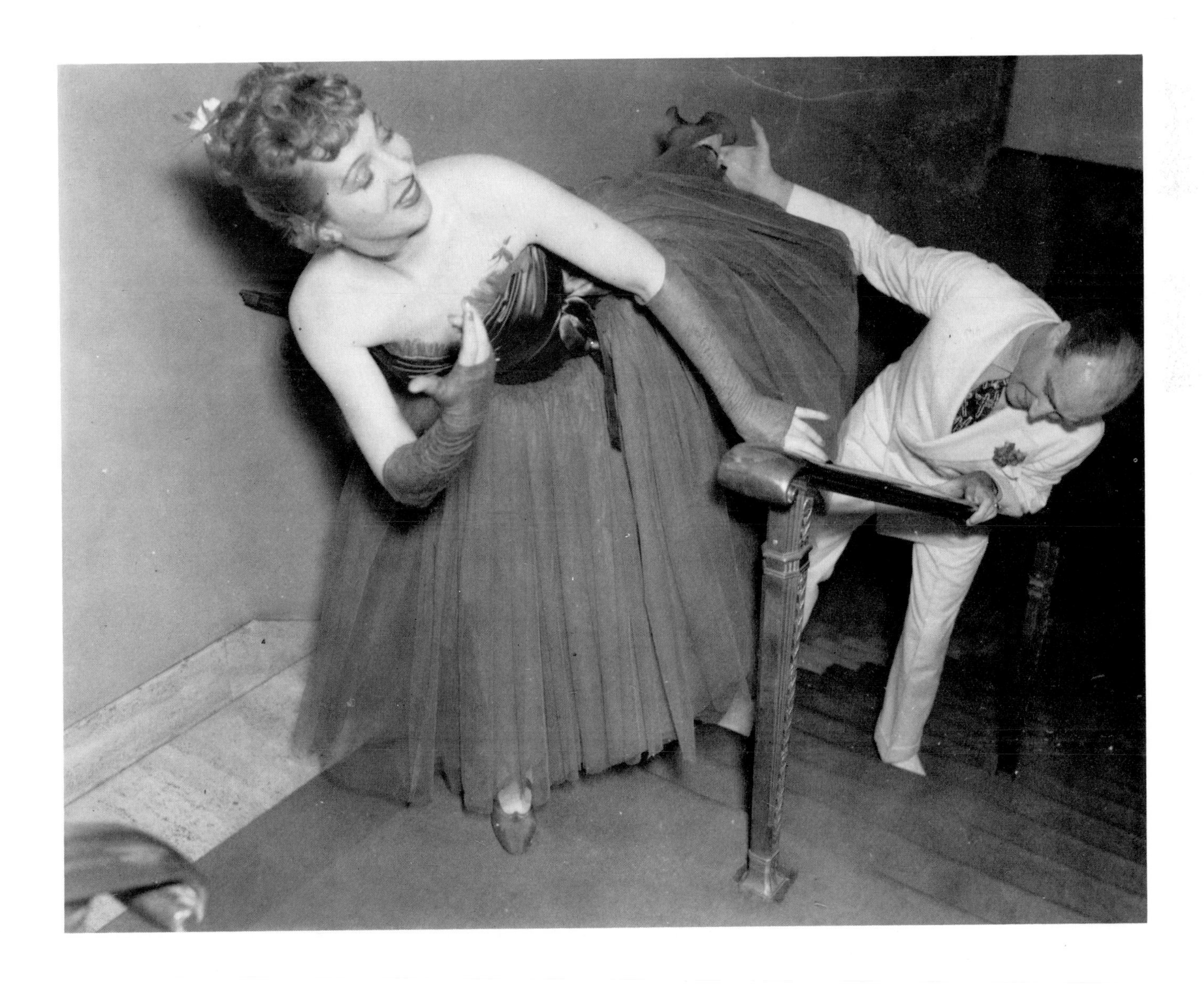

ON THE FACING PAGE, *Jacques Fath and Paulette Goddard. Miss Goddard has made herself up to resemble Joan Crawford, and Jacques Fath intended to resemble Maurice Chevalier, but he comes closer to resembling Buster Keaton.*

BELOW, *Gene Tierney and the Aly Khan. Having told Zerbe many times that he dreaded growing old, he may have been readier than most men to die at forty-nine.*

At Peggy Guggenheim's, in Venice. ABOVE, LEFT, *a view across the canal to the Gritti-Palace.* BELOW, LEFT, *a bronze by Marini.* ON THE FACING PAGE, *the sage collector.*

ABOVE, *Ingrid Bergman and her Rossellini children.*

ON THE FACING PAGE, *Sacha Guitry at Versailles.*

One day in the country, Paul Draper took it into his head to float in air.

Lincoln Kirstein and companion.

A visit to Saint Briavel, Natalie Hays Hammond's Elizabethan manor house high on the rocks above Gloucester harbor. RIGHT, *the dancer Francesca Braggiotti skimming above the beach.* BELOW, RIGHT, *Zerbe momentarily transformed by Miss Braggiotti's golden tresses.* BELOW, LEFT, *Dinah, a friend of Miss Hammond.*

LEFT, *Miss Braggiotti pretending to be a movie starlet.* BELOW, LEFT, *Miss Hammond in a dress made for her mother by Worth of Paris, at the time of Queen Victoria's Diamond Jubilee.* BELOW, *Miss Hammond with three other friends, in the garden at Saint Briavel.*

The august and able newspaper columnist and historian Mark Sullivan, during a visit to Henry Luce's plantation at Mepkin, South Carolina. The newspaperman who was least like Sullivan and whom Sullivan would least like to have met faces him ON THE OPPOSITE PAGE.

The scandalmongering tabloid gossip columnist and high-pitched, machine-gun-like, rat-tat-tat radio commentator Walter Winchell, who addressed himself to "Mr. and Mrs. North America and all the ships at sea," and who found his audiences willing to believe almost everything he told them. A former vaudeville hoofer, Winchell had intelligence, energy, and incomparable chutzpah. *As the Second World War approached, his attacks on Nazi Germany proved useful to President Roosevelt, who, not being a fastidious man, had no difficulty calling him Walter.*

ABOVE, *Margaret Bourke-White.*

LEFT, *John Gielgud.*

ON THE FACING PAGE, *Serge Obolensky and Gertrude Lawrence on Cecil Beaton's bed at the St. Regis.*

The Duke of Windsor at the Homestead, White Sulphur Springs. In the UPPER PICTURE, *he seems unexpectedly waiflike as he glances over toward Senator Stuart Symington, busily totting up his golf score. In the* LOWER PICTURE, *the Duke is plainly more in his element, playing traps in Meyer Davis's band.*

Stopping off in Jamaica on his way home to England from a visit to the United States, Sir Winston Churchill was persuaded by his friend Zerbe to walk down onto the shore one evening and have his picture taken against the setting sun; see FACING PAGE. *Because of the uncertain light, Zerbe used a flashbulb, which led to an extraordinary effect—shadows that run in opposite directions simultaneously. Picture-taking over, Sir Winston marched off to have dinner with Zerbe, paying no heed to his soiled clothes. The fact is, he was hungry and thirsty.*

Rarely in history can so many beautiful women have been gathered into a single room (to say nothing of being willing to sit together long enough to have their likenesses taken). In the usual order, ABOVE, *are Ina Claire, Paulette Goddard, Valentina, the then Mrs. Vincent Astor, Lorraine Dresselhuys, Constance Woodsworth, Mrs. William Rhinelander Stewart, Irene Selznick, Mrs. Alfred de Liagre, Jr., and Mrs. Michael Arlen.*

ON THE FACING PAGE, *a dinner party given by Dr. Gaylord Hauser for the King and Queen of Yugoslavia. Seated, Mrs. Geoffrey Gates, Dr. Hauser, the Queen; standing, Mrs. Kingman Douglass (Adele Astaire), the King, and Paulette Goddard.*

Zerbe has an artist's sharp eye for resemblances in things that look at first glance very different. ABOVE, *the stone hounds in the gardens of the palace at Caserta, near Naples, are not unlike a fashion shot that he took of some models in Bermuda,* OPPOSITE, ABOVE, *many years earlier. The ancient circus wagon that he photographed in Florida is similar in spirit to the hearse,* OPPOSITE, *which the Japanese on Okinawa ingeniously affixed to the chassis of an old American Hudson.*

Architecture makes an admirable avocation for a photographer—among other reasons, because he is always in its presence. In Zerbe's case, within this general avocation he has specialized in the eccentric and amusing. He favors pavilions and follies and has a soft spot in his heart for fanciful rooms that recall another time. ON THIS PAGE, ABOVE, *a Gothic Revival room in the English home of the dress designer Norman Hartnell.* BELOW, *a bathroom in the house of Mrs. Paul Fagan, in Pebble Beach. Much of the detail is authentic medieval stonework; the sink is a baptismal font.*

ON THE FACING PAGE, ABOVE, *a bedroom in Beverly Hills, and,* BELOW, *the men's room in the Casino at Newport. The pagan richness of the design, executed in 1879–1881 by McKim, Mead & White, is very much at odds with our usual notion of proper Victorian taste.*

Everything else being equal, Zerbe has always preferred a complex opulence to simplicity, but he has been enough of a historian to compile a photographic record of both. ON THE FACING PAGE, ABOVE, *an ancient house in Key West, long since torn down;* BELOW, *a cast iron fence in Key West, happily preserved. The balusters are in the form of ripening cornstalks.*

ABOVE, *a libidinous tree growing near the front door of the Jules Bache house in Palm Beach.* BELOW, *Mr. Bache at lunch. Bache was a big man in Wall Street. He had a butler who was known to be at least as clever about money as his master. Sometimes over brandy and cigars Bache would recommend a certain stock to his guests, and the butler, standing with suitable deference behind his master's chair, would gravely shake his head in silent veto.*

As people grow older, they tend to abandon novels in favor of essays and biographies; as photographers grow older, they tend to abandon people in favor of buildings and nature. ON THE FACING PAGE, *an old mill being made over into a house, near Bedford Village, New York.* ON THIS PAGE, *William Randolph Hearst's Cinderella house in McCloud, California, and a High Victorian mansion in Rhinebeck, New York, a Hudson River town where Zerbe used to visit his friend Vincent Astor. Astor also had a place in Bermuda, through the grounds of which he enjoyed driving a narrow-gauge railway train.*

Architects who work in a traditional vein have always laid great store by the enfilade, a procession of great rooms that open one into the other, giving delight to the eye and making it easy to entertain on a substantial scale. ON THE FACING PAGE, ABOVE, *the enfilade, which seems to approach infinity, at New Place, the Crocker family home in Burlingame, California. Some architects and interior decorators have clients notably bloodthirsty in their tastes.* BELOW, LEFT, *a grisly drawing room in the Château de la Celles les Bords, and,* AT RIGHT, *trophies in the McMartin House, in Bermuda.* ON THIS PAGE, *a room at Blenheim. The only animals present are painted, woven, or carved.*

ABOVE, *a street scene in Florence.* ON THE FACING PAGE, ABOVE, *the Dolmabahçe Palace, in Istanbul, and,* BELOW, *the summer pavilion of the Topkapi Palace.*

ON THE FACING PAGE, *Dali at the house of Paul-Louis Weiller, outside Paris. Dali had asked if he might bring a girl to lunch; the next day it was learned, to the wonder of the other guests, that his exquisite companion had been a boy.*

ON THIS PAGE, *Anthony Perkins outside a fashionable New York restaurant, and Ginger Rogers flying to Paris and doing ample homework en route.*

ON THE FACING PAGE, *at the Gibson Girl Ball, held at the Plaza, two old beauties and two young ones. In the* UPPER PICTURE *are Mrs. Charles Dana Gibson, who had been her husband's model for the earliest drawings of the Gibson Girl, and Mrs. Harvey Cushing, formidable mother of three much sought-after Cushing girls;* LOWER, *Mrs. Oleg Cassini and Gene Tierney. It was to be seen in their faces that years would not turn them into Mrs. Gibson and Mrs. Cushing.*

ON THIS PAGE, *Mrs. Joseph Neff admires the voluptuous nymph by Canova that she presented to the Metropolitan Museum.* BELOW *is a sleeping hermaphrodite in the Villa Borghese, in Rome.*

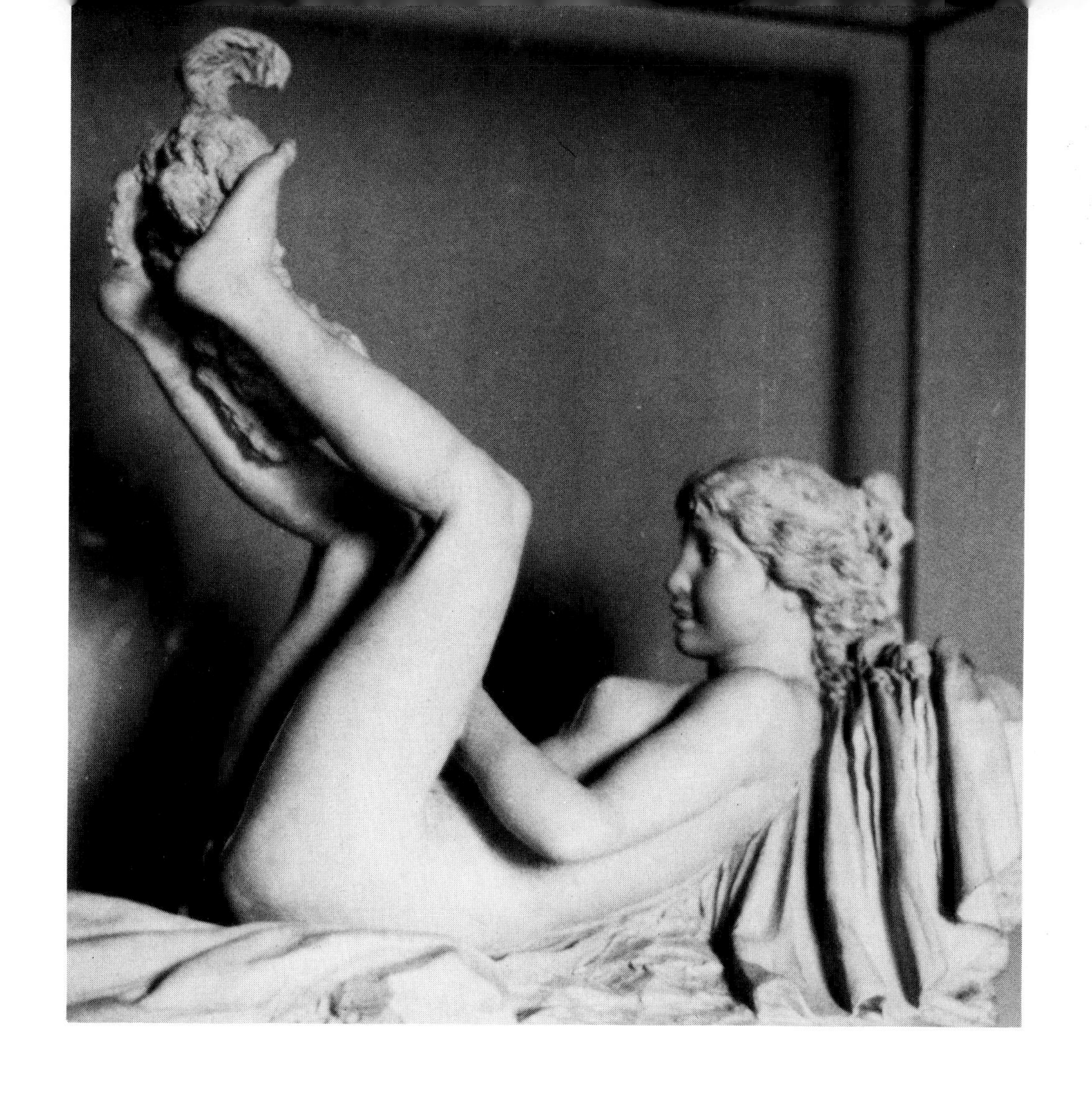

Zerbe has an eye for architectural detail; also an eye for pranks. Over the years, he has collected an impressive number of pictures of people in unexpected positions, some posed and some not. ABOVE, *Fanny Brice showing off in her pool in Hollywood.* BELOW, *the opera singer Lawrence Tibbett revealing the abrasions he suffered when he boyishly attempted to leap over a hedge.* ON THE FACING PAGE, ABOVE, *the pretty girl frolicking with a squirrel is not flesh and blood, but a statue by Clodion; the girl* BELOW *is real and evidently in high spirits.*

At parties in Cleveland forty years ago, Zerbe would get his friends to form surprising photographic patterns. ABOVE, LEFT, *a clock group. At about four-thirty, in the dress with fringe, is Kay Halle, now a celebrated Washington hostess.* BELOW, *young Philip Johnson and his sister Theodate trying out a sofa of advanced design. As an architect, Johnson was later to incorporate playfulness into his plans with the help of pools, fountains, statuary, carpeted walls, and, at his place in New Canaan, an arched folly just too low to stand up in. As for Zerbe's playfulness, it has always required a considerable amount of physical stamina.* ON THE FACING PAGE, *he dances the twist with Hermione Gingold at the Drake.* ON THIS PAGE, ABOVE, RIGHT, *a harmless tumble while playing musical chairs at the St. Regis.*

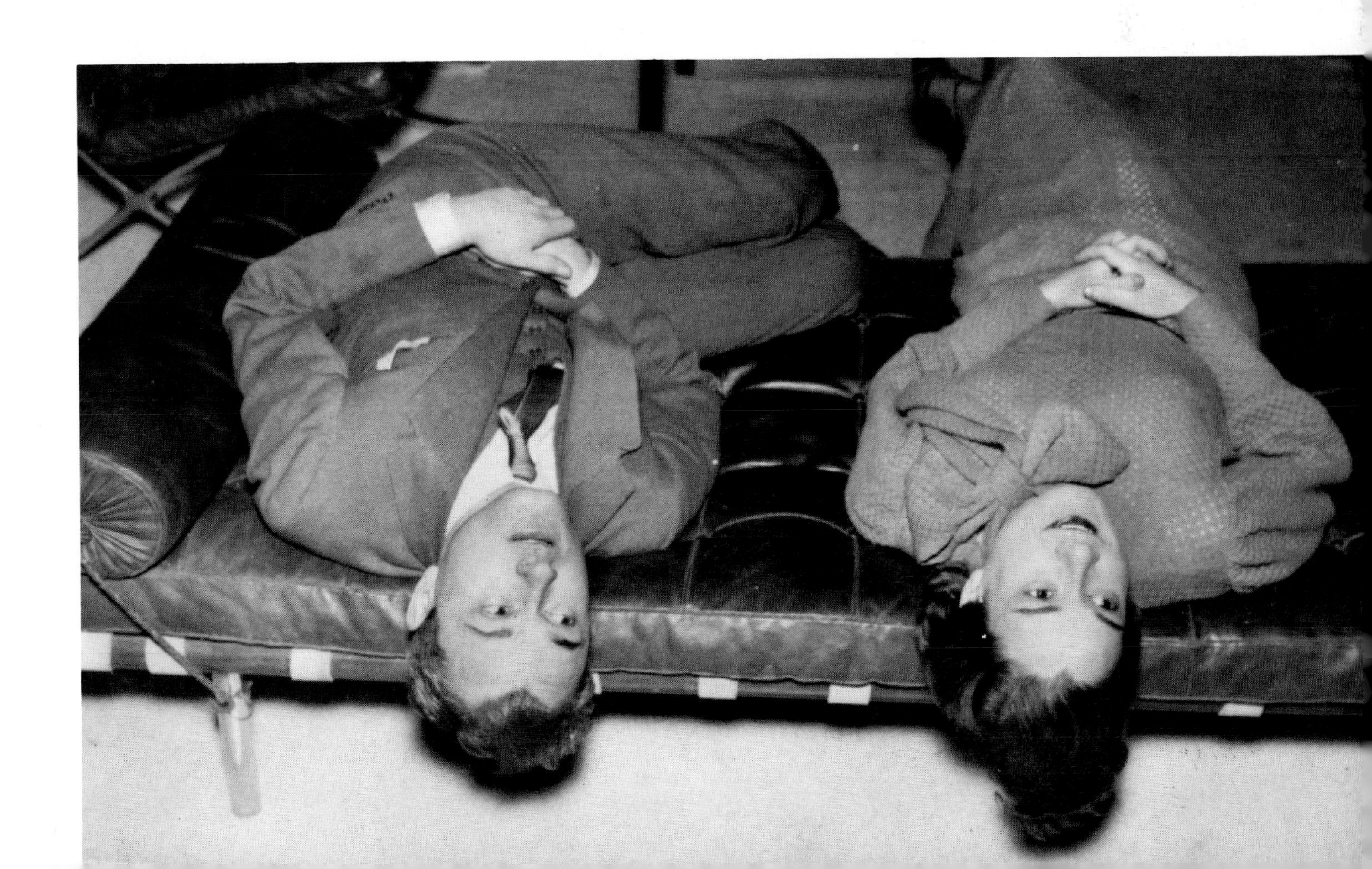

A shower at Hedda's; among the ladies are Ethel Barrymore, Gene Tierney, Shirley Temple, June Allyson, Mrs. Gary Cooper, Mona Freeman, Jean Peters, and Joan Evans. ON THE FACING PAGE, *the celebrated raconteur Sammy Colt delivering his mother to the party.* BELOW, *George Cukor's house.*

More patterns, more pranks. ON THE FACING PAGE, ABOVE, *a gathering in Hollywood; among those at the party is Kirk Douglas.* BELOW, *a friend of Zerbe's floating underwater and apparently in no haste to surface.* ON THIS PAGE, ABOVE, *more partygoing: the Gary Coopers and the Humphrey Bogarts; and,* BELOW, *Cooper and Jimmy Stewart.*

On the set of Around the World in Eighty Days. BELOW, *David Niven, Cantinflas, Marlene Dietrich, Frank Sinatra, George Raft, and Red Skelton. Zerbe was a close friend of Mike Todd. He was often tempted to try his hand at acting in movies, and Todd assured him that* Around the World in Eighty Days *would be as good a place to start as any—it had a cast of thousands, not all of them competent. As things turned out, Zerbe put off his movie debut until 1973, when he starred in* The House of Seven Gables.

BAR

THIS END UP
LAMP BULBS
GLASS
HANDLE
WITH CARE

Mainbocher taking his ease in Hollywood. AT RIGHT, BELOW, *some creatures do likewise.* AT RIGHT, ABOVE, *Joseph Cotten, Elsa Maxwell, and Rita Hayworth playing peekaboo behind a masterly sculpture in ice.*

Zerbe has been visiting Paris regularly for fifty years. As a young man just out of Yale, he was photographed, FACING PAGE, BELOW, *by his friend George Hoynigen-Huene on the balcony of his flat overlooking the Boulevard Saint-Germain.* ABOVE, *drawing class at the Académie Julian, which Zerbe attended but did not frequent. When, after a decade's absence, he dropped in one day at the Académie, the head teacher exclaimed, "My dear fellow! Where on earth* were *you last year?"* ON THIS PAGE, *the Place de la Concorde seemingly sinking underwater.*

ON THE FACING PAGE, ABOVE, *fireworks beyond Notre Dame. The picture was taken from the penthouse terrace of Zerbe's old friend Mrs. Tassos Fondaras, on the Ile Saint-Louis.* BELOW, *Jack Lemmon, Audrey Hepburn, and William Holden in Paris to make a movie. It was called* Paris When It Sizzles, *and it was not a success.*

ON THIS PAGE, ABOVE, *Yves Montand and Marilyn Monroe, when they were starring in* Let's Make Love. BELOW, *Miss Monroe signing her autograph while the former United States Ambassador to the Court of St. James's, Winthrop Aldrich, thinks of something to say to her.*

Zerbe has never played any sport and is not ordinarily thought of by his friends as a man eager to rise early and be out among horses and dogs. Nevertheless, he has occasionally done so, and to great photographic effect. ABOVE, *the stables at Saratoga on a frosty morning.* ON THE FACING PAGE, ABOVE, *a drag at Aiken, and hunting in the Chagrin Valley;* BELOW, *jockeys getting a better look.*

ON THE FACING PAGE, ABOVE, *a plantation in Louisiana. In the eighteenth and early nineteenth centuries, no matter how grand a plantation house might be, the avenue approaching it was often impassable, especially in winter; most guests took care to come by water and not overland. On the garden axis,* BELOW, *a handsome Greek Revival double outhouse, with charming hearts carved in the doors.* ON THIS PAGE, *the Mississippi approaches the top of a levee.*

IN MEMORY OF
THOMAS ROMER
BORN IN NASSAU
N.P 1783
DIED AT KEY
FLA SEP 8
AGED 108

Among Zerbe's lifelong preoccupations has been the photographing of gravestones, particularly the gravestones in abandoned cemeteries, where one must often look twice to see them tilted askew in the high grass or in a thicket of wild raspberries.

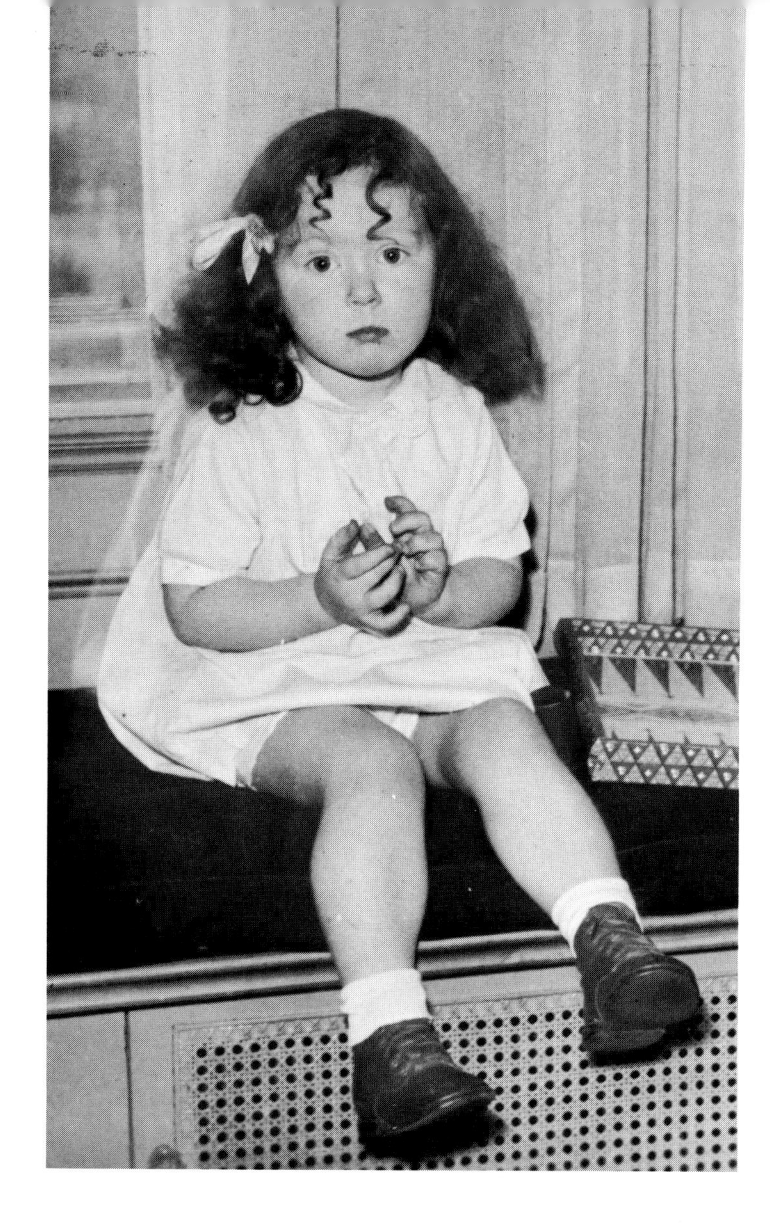

Zerbe has also been an able photographer of children. TO THE RIGHT, *a gamine in Cleveland.* BELOW, *the Gorgas children, of Birmingham, and Master Antone Charles Steuver, Jr., of St. Louis.* ON THE FACING PAGE, *Amanda Mortimer, of New York, who was to become the well-known beauty Amanda Burden.*

ON THE FACING PAGE, *a boy and his dog somewhere in Switzerland; Victoria Kelly, daughter of Brenda Frazier Kelly and John ("Shipwreck") Kelly, attends the dancing classes of Willie de Rham, at the Colony Club; Victoria and her mother celebrate a sixth-birthday anniversary (one of the candles on the cake is "to grow on"); and in the Palm Court of the Plaza, a young father, perhaps newly divorced, proudly entertains his daughter, whose attention has drifted elsewhere.* BELOW, *some boys in Bermuda, dressed in what they described as "Indian mud regalia."*

Zerbe was glad to visit Frank Lloyd Wright and to photograph him, but he has no patience with Wright's kind of architecture. Zerbe once described Taliesen West as being in the "tutti-frutti" style, and he said of the clients for whom Wright built houses that they were "people who had no past and plainly expected no future." TO THE LEFT, *a monumental sculpture at Taliesen West, and,* BELOW, *a high-tension pylon in the neighborhood.* ON THE FACING PAGE, *the old Master taking the sun.*

Among the buildings that satisfy Zerbe's taste for the eccentric is the castle AT LEFT, ABOVE, *built by the actor William Gillette high above the Connecticut River near Hadlyme. (In his will, Gillette commanded his executors not to sell the castle to some unappreciative "blithering saphead." Since only a blithering saphead—whatever that highly subjective term might mean—would be likely to purchase such a structure, to say nothing of building it, a legal impasse resulted. It was resolved when the State of Connecticut decided to purchase the property for use as a state park.) In County Kildare, Ireland, hard by Castletown House, stands Mrs. "Speaker" Conolly's so-called Wonderful Barn,* ABOVE. *It was built to give employment to the poor during hard times.* TO THE LEFT *sits Henry McIlhenny, of Philadelphia, outside his castle, Glenveagh, in County Donegal; he is enjoying that Irish curiosity, sunlight.* ON THE FACING PAGE, *a view of Glenveagh on its dark bright mountain shore.*

ABOVE, LEFT, *the old monks' walk at Lismore Castle, Ireland;* ABOVE, RIGHT, *nuns at Bruges.* BELOW, LEFT, *stacking hay in the Alpes-Maritimes;* BELOW, RIGHT, *daffodils along the Hudson at Rhinebeck.* ON THE FACING PAGE, *a runaway horse from a merry-go-round. When Zerbe photographed him, he was heading west through Indiana.*

ON THE FACING PAGE, ABOVE, *the Liffey at Dublin;* BELOW, LEFT, *Luttrellstown Castle, in County Dublin;* BELOW, RIGHT, *luncheon at Luttrellstown, and* ON THIS PAGE, *a view of its great park.*

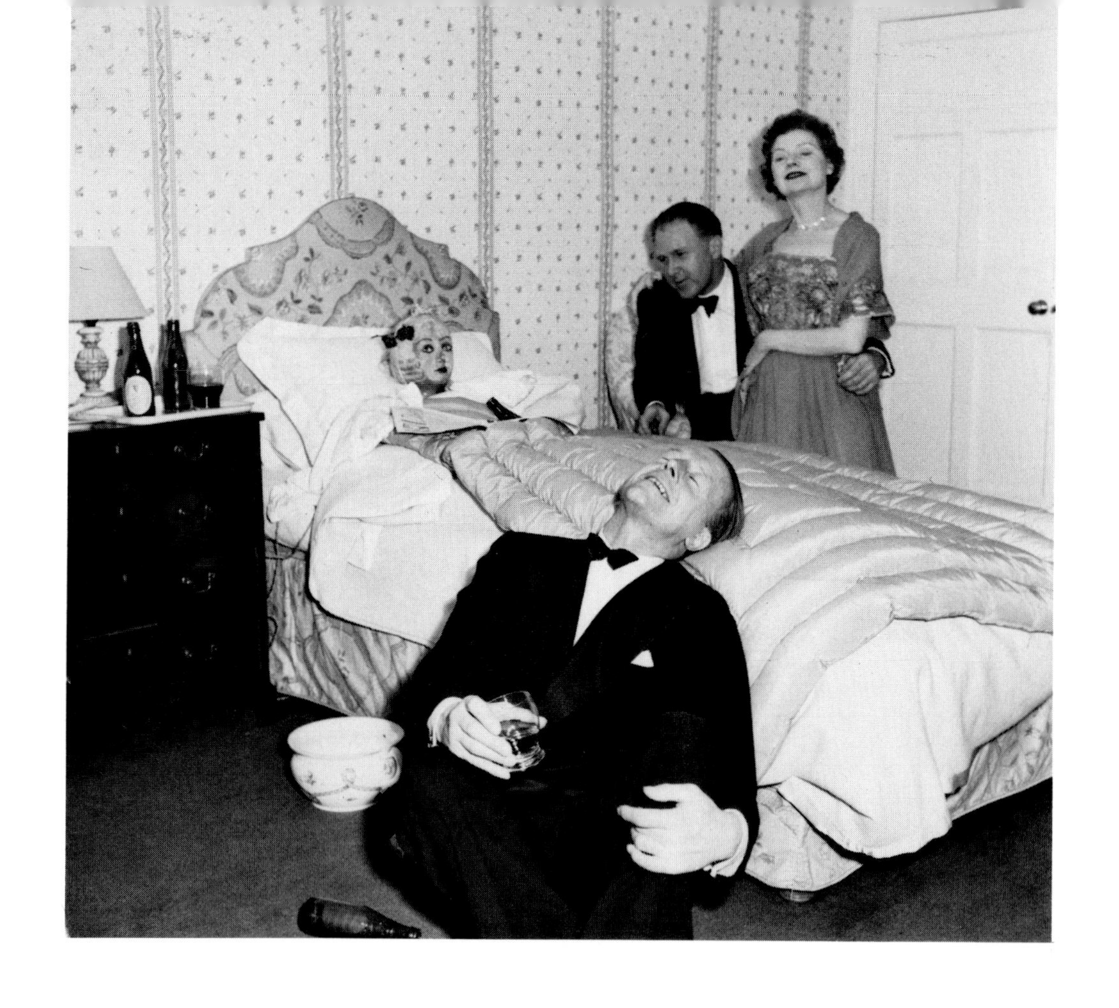

ON THE FACING PAGE, ABOVE, *a bedtime prank at Luttrellstown. The mannequin is gravely ill, but it is hoped by Roderick More O'Farrell, Felix Harbord, and their hostess at Luttrellstown, Aileen Plunket, that repeated applications of Guinness will bring her round. Mrs. Plunket is herself a Guinness.* BELOW, *Mrs. Kingman Douglass (Adele Astaire) at home in Ireland.*

ON THIS PAGE, *Mr. and Mrs. John Philip Cohane and their children at Holly Park, County Limerick.*

Mariga Guinness, wife of the Honorable Desmond Guinness and, with him, the force that drives the Irish Georgian Society. The purpose of the society is to preserve those noble houses, parks, squares, and follies that were the pride of the Ascendancy in the eighteenth century and that the ordinary citizens of Ireland are today eager to see fall into ruin. OPPOSITE, *John Huston, citizen of Ireland and former joint master of the Galway Blazers.*

From the moment when, as a schoolboy, Zerbe first visited Madame Du Barry's pavilion at Louveciennes, pictured AT THE TOP OF THE FACING PAGE *in a contemporary print, he has been agreeably haunted by her life. The pool,* BELOW, *which lies hidden in a long-overgrown garden, is one by which Du Barry used to sit.*

ON THIS PAGE, ABOVE, *an inaccurate but fetching likeness of Du Barry.* BELOW, RIGHT, *a bust of her husband, the accommodating Marquis;* ON THE LEFT, *two eighteenth-century busts of Madame in terra cotta, which Zerbe had in his collection and which he has presented to the Louvre, for exhibition at Versailles.*

ON THE FACING PAGE, ABOVE, LEFT, *the hole in the window at Versailles through which Louis XVI is said to have poked his telescope in order to see who was coming up the avenue.* AT RIGHT, *the pavilion at Bidaine.* BELOW, *not all the châteaux that Zerbe admires are in France; this one is Biltmore House, in the Great Smoky Mountains of western North Carolina. Its builder, George Vanderbilt, had intended to put up a modest shooting box, but his architect, Richard Morris Hunt, knew better.*

ON THIS PAGE, ABOVE, LEFT, *the Grand Trianon at Versailles;* ABOVE, RIGHT, *a ruinous stairway at Le Desert de Retz, Chambourcy.* BELOW, LEFT, *the Gothic folly at Frampton;* BELOW, RIGHT, *an old German folk song, from which Cole Porter borrowed the idea for his joyous "Let's Do It, Let's Fall in Love."*

ON THE FACING PAGE, *Cyril Connolly in Paris, while Zerbe and he were preparing their book on pavilions; Nancy Mitford outside her house in Paris; and W. Somerset Maugham, in extreme old age, at his Villa Mauresque.* ON THIS PAGE, *tea at Mrs. Ian Fleming's, in London. Cyril Connolly and Lady Diana Cooper standing, and Anne Fleming seated on the hearth.*

In 1933, Alfred Lunt, Lynn Fontanne, and Noël Coward came to Cleveland to play in Design for Living, *and their friend Zerbe went backstage to take these photographs of them.*

ON THE FACING PAGE, *the quintessential Coward. The occasion was the Allied War Relief Ball, given during the early years of the Second World War. For a long time, Coward seemed much younger than his years; with sickness, he grew prematurely old, and he once described himself, not without relish, as looking like an elderly, diseased Chinese mandarin.* ON THIS PAGE, *glimpses of Coward with Beatrice Lillie and, much later, with a friend at Firefly, his villa in Jamaica, where, early in 1973, having morning coffee, he died.* ABOVE, *the Lunts with Vivien Leigh; and a notable table: Bert Lahr, Ethel Merman, the producer Richard Aldrich, Gertrude Lawrence (who was Mrs. Aldrich), and Coward.*

The Lunts at dinner at Whitney Warren's house in San Francisco. Lynn Fontanne illustrates an anecdote as a waiter pours champagne. The lady at Lunt's left, ABOVE, *is Ina Claire, whose guardian when she was a child was one of Zerbe's uncles.*

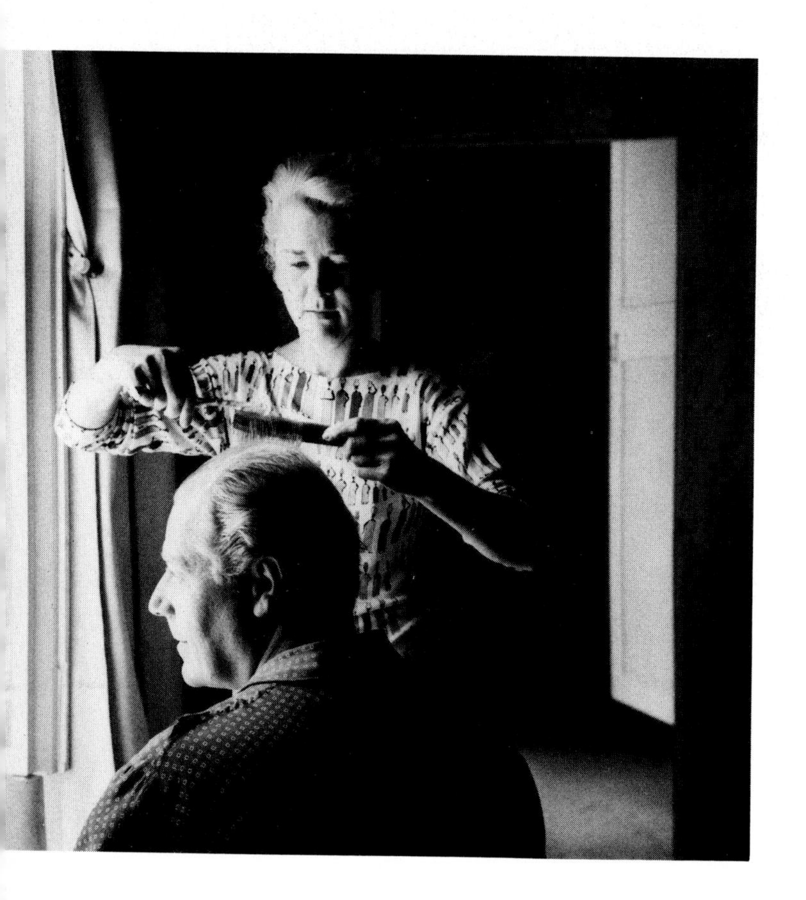

Some European aristocrats. ON THIS PAGE, *the Archduke Franz Josef of Austria and his wife, Martha, at Miami Beach; Serge Obolensky, bewigged; Alexander Hohenlohe having his hair cut by his wife, Honey, at Schloss Mittersill; and King George of Greece.* ON THE FACING PAGE, *Prince Potenziani of Rome.*

American aristocrats. One perceives that their distinguishing characteristic is not beauty but confidence. ABOVE, *Eric Hatch contentedly pours himself what is plainly not a first or second glass of champagne.* ON THE FACING PAGE *are John Jacob Astor II; Jay Rutherfurd with Mrs. Vincent Astor (later to be Mrs. Lytle Hull); Mrs. Cornelius Vanderbilt, in her famous headache band, standing between Geoffrey Parsons, editor of the New York* Herald Tribune, *and Alice Roosevelt Longworth; and* la Duchesse de Talleyrand et Perigord, *who had been born Helen Gould, of Tarrytown, New York.*

ON THE FACING PAGE, ABOVE, *Mr. and Mrs. David Wagstaff looking content with themselves.* BELOW, *Mrs. Evalyn Walsh McLean entertaining at Friendship, in Washington, D.C. The sofa speaks louder than words.*

ON THIS PAGE, *Nutwood Farm, in Cleveland, a long time ago. One is surprised to note that the girl in the picture, Petsey Winslow, is smoking.*

For Town & Country, *Zerbe took photographs of many hundreds of debuts.* ON THE FACING PAGE, ABOVE, *is a picture of a girl named Glenna Gardiner, at the annual Tuxedo Ball.* ABOVE, *Helena Wolfe and her father, Dr. Paul Austin Wolfe, rector of the Brick Church.* AT LEFT, *some views of a popular debutante, Jacqueline Bouvier.*

The second Mrs. Vincent Astor.

ON THE FACING PAGE, *Mrs. Astor's dachshunds, Robin and Pickle.*

From a photographer's point of view, the most amusing parties to cover are those to which people come in costume—the attempt to be other than who one is lends a touch of the pagan to the sternest puritan. ON THE FACING PAGE, *a ball in Dallas; everyone looks content but circumspect in his ordinary evening dress. Save for a couple in the right foreground, who appear to be sitting on the floor, nothing surprising is likely to take place throughout the evening; at a costume party, one would have higher hopes.* ABOVE, *a couple of people who have brightened costume balls in many countries: on the left is Cecil Beaton, and on the right is Mrs. Harrison Williams, whose escort has given less thought to his costume than Mr. Beaton did. Mrs. Williams looks understandably disappointed.*

above, *Elsa Maxwell holding court at an April-in-Paris Ball at the Waldorf. If the figure on the right is Cardinal Richelieu, then Miss Maxwell is no less a person than Marie de Médicis. But the periods are mingled, for the couple at the left is plainly intended to represent Napoleon and Josephine.*

AT RIGHT, *Sandra Payson in her young beauty at a come-as-a-book party held at her parents' home in Manhasset. Her companion, John Coleman, may be Little Red Riding Hood's grandmother or perhaps even Little Red Riding Hood herself. In any case, his shoes are unconvincing.*

ON THE FACING PAGE, ABOVE, *Elsa Maxwell and Clifton Webb.* BELOW, *on a statelier occasion, Tilly Losch, Ezio Pinza, Gloria Swanson, and Maggie McNellis—figures not often encountered in hotel elevators.*

People in costume. TO THE RIGHT, *Florence Cagle and Zerbe showing off with an unidentified third party.* BELOW, LEFT, *Gary Cooper looking somewhat more El Moroccan than Moroccan, and,* BELOW, RIGHT, *the Duke of Marlborough and Mrs. Gary Cooper; the Duke makes a thoroughly implausible pirate.* ON THE FACING PAGE, ABOVE, *Gloria Swanson at a shipboard party gives her well-known impersonation of an old friend. The master of ceremonies urging her on is Earl Blackwell, who appears to believe he is Rembrandt.* BELOW, *Lillian Gish at her own costume party; the theme of the evening, to judge by Miss Gish, must have been patriotic.*

ABOVE, *the debut of Mary MacArthur. In the reception line with her are her mother, Helen Hayes, and her father, Charles MacArthur.* BELOW, *Audrey Hepburn greeting Doris and Jean Stein at Jean Stein's debut.*

ABOVE, at the debut of his daughter Barbara, the movie producer Jack Warner demonstrates to Eric Loder that his tail coat is twelve years old. BELOW, Judy Garland congratulates Louise and Barbara Warner.

For Town & Country, *Zerbe photographed at least as many weddings as he did debuts.* ABOVE, *Ann Firestone getting ready for the ceremony. She appears to have thought of everything, including the then obligatory garter.* ABOVE, RIGHT, *the bride being dressed by Mr. John, the hatmaker.*

RIGHT, *the first postnuptial kiss.* ON THE FACING PAGE, *the reception in the big striped tent and the fun of meeting all those middle-aged people who went to Yale and Smith with one's parents.*

An especially happy occasion: the marriage, in the summer of 1947, of Barbara ("Babe") Cushing Mortimer to William S. Paley. The setting was the Paley country place on Long Island. In the midst of the handsome family group ON THE FACING PAGE *sits Mrs. Harvey Cushing, with her two Mortimer grandchildren, Stanley and Amanda. Two other grandchildren, Kate and Sara Whitney, are seated on the lawn. (Their mother, who had been Betsey Cushing, was married first to their father, James Roosevelt, and then to John Hay Whitney, who adopted them.) Standing are, in the usual order, Mr. and Mrs. Harvey Cushing II, Mrs. Vincent Astor (the former Mary Cushing, who subsequently became Mrs. James Forsburgh), Vincent Astor, the bridegroom and bride, and Jock and Betsey Whitney.* BELOW *are Mrs. Whitney's dachshund, resting in a chair whose decay admirably accommodates his short legs, and the bride an hour before the ceremony.* ON THIS PAGE, *feeding the bride; frightening the bridegroom; the celebrated radio and TV personality Ed Murrow with Jock Whitney; and the Whitneys at the end of a long, merry day.*

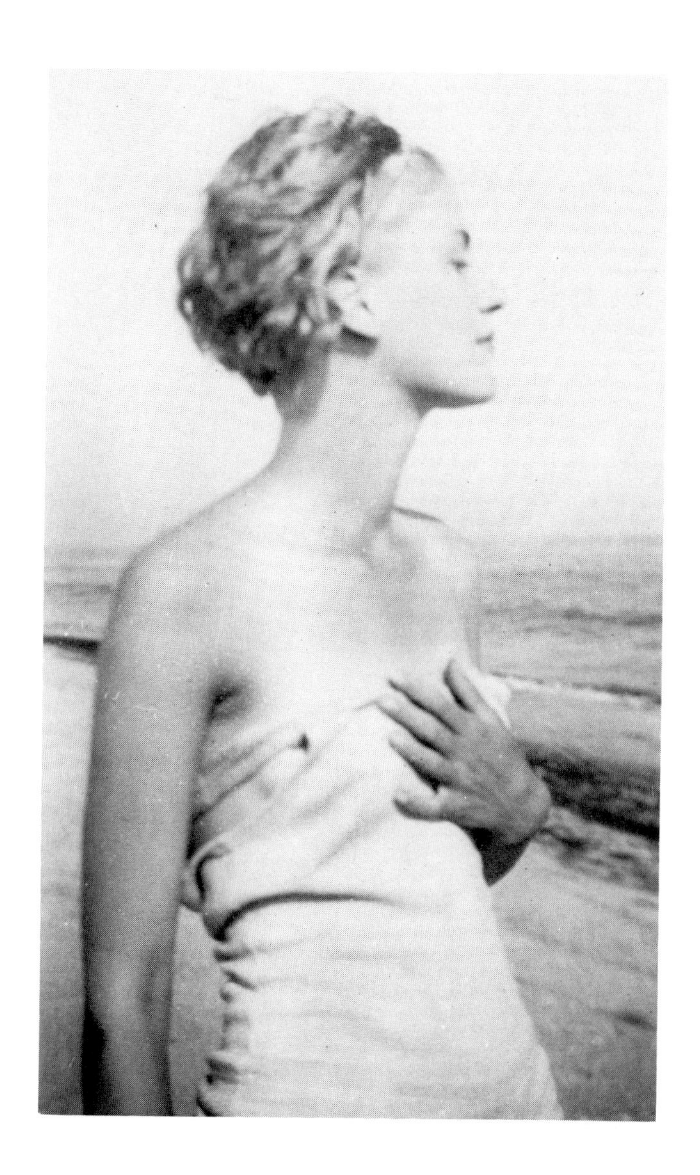

For even longer than he has been paying visits to Paris, Zerbe has been visiting Nantucket. ON THE OPPOSITE PAGE, TOP, *a specimen of island horseplay and a pretty girl sunning herself on the beach. Her wool bathing suit is of the kind that used to take hours to dry—one would have to pull it on clammily wet and cold for the second dip of the day.* AT BOTTOM, *an early Brownie shot of Main Street. Fifty years later, the hitching post is still in place.* ON THIS PAGE, *a view of Centre Street at twenty-two minutes after eleven on a fine summer's morning.*

Nantucket clambakes. The lady under the table is Zerbe's mother, taking shelter from a sudden shower.

Cocktails. ON THE FACING PAGE, *summertime on Nantucket and under the parasol, of course in a hat, sits Zerbe's mother, in her vigorous eighties.* ON THIS PAGE, RIGHT, *Hedda Hopper greeting Judy Garland at a party in New York, and,* BELOW, *Janet Blair greeting Marion Davies at a party in Hollywood. This is perhaps the last picture ever taken of Miss Davies.*

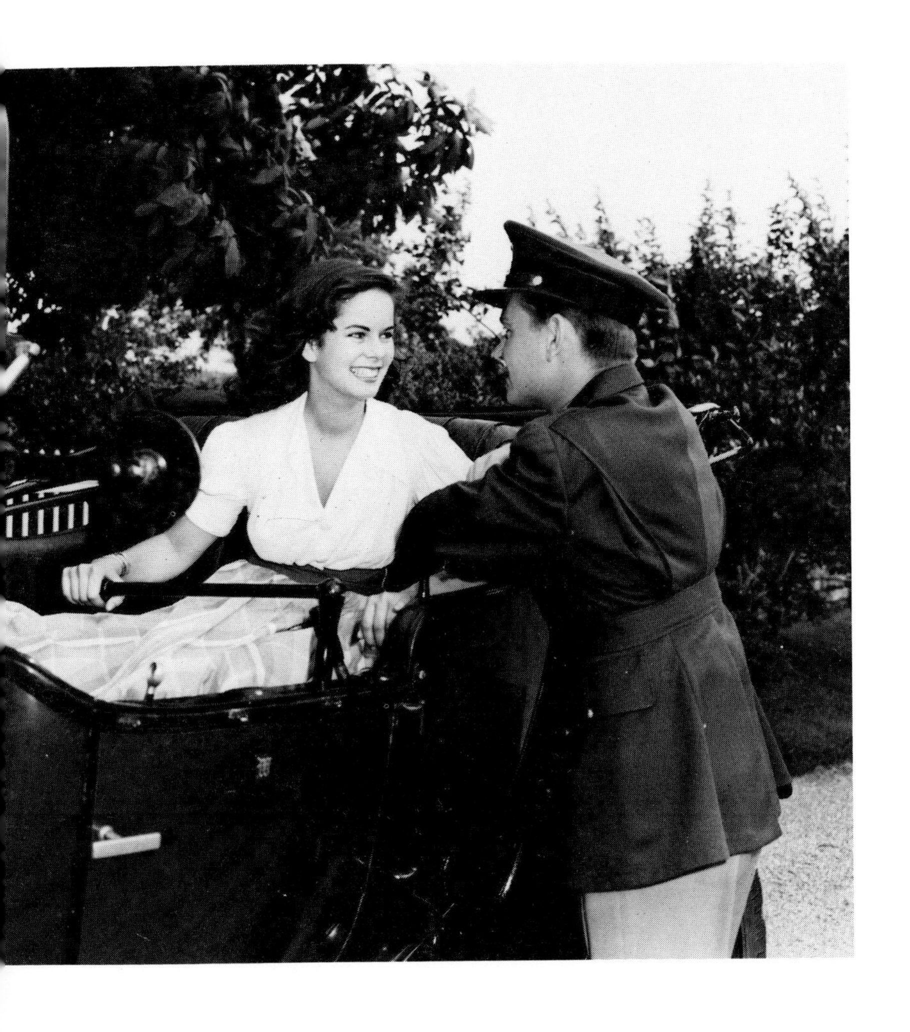

While still in her teens, Oona O'Neill posed for one of a series of advertisements that Zerbe prepared for Jergens Lotion. A year or so later, she was to marry Charlie Chaplin. Most of these pictures were taken for fun and not in order to sell anything.

Over the years, Zerbe has tried his hand at both advertising and fashion photography. AT TOP, *an early White Rock advertisement, the models being his friends Beatrice Lillie and Paul Draper.* BELOW, *Zerbe's friends Lillian O'Donnell and Robert McIlwaine posing for a Jergens Lotion ad on the handsome bronze stairway of the St. Regis, and Gigi de Terwangne modeling a dress at Versailles.* ON THE FACING PAGE, *Simonetta Visconti Fabiana stands sternly awhirl on the Spanish Steps.*

More and more in recent years, Zerbe has devoted himself to photographing buildings and places. ON THIS PAGE, *a monkey in Bou Saada, Morocco, warning passers-by that he bites; and the triumphal arch leading into the Hermitage Palace, in Leningrad.* ON THE FACING PAGE, *the billiards room of the Oranienbaum Palace, in Russia, and the third-floor back stairs of Arkangelskoye, a Russian country estate. If one didn't know that the stairway was of the eighteenth century, one would assume that it was the handiwork of some promising young Scandinavian architect of the late twentieth.*

Zerbe continues to take pictures for Town & Country. ON THE FACING PAGE, ABOVE, *Prince Egon von Furstenberg and Sloan Simpson.* BELOW, *also, an ostrich that happened to take Zerbe's fancy and a snapshot of Zerbe with his old friend Millie Considine.*

ABOVE, *since his school days, Zerbe has flirted with the notion of becoming a professional actor. He realized this ambition in 1973, when he starred in a movie version of* The House of Seven Gables. *He played the part of Clifford Pyncheon, a man who spent thirty years in prison for a crime he didn't commit. Though he disliked himself in the role, his performance was much praised.*

Zerbe in Acapulco in 1973.

INDEX

Figures in italics indicate pages upon which pictures occur.

Lillie
ESLIE BRIC
CONST
CARPENTER
ES CLARE
HE PIANOS
ADIE
GÉRARD